The
ROYAL AIR FORCE
of
WORLD WAR TWO
in color

The
ROYAL AIR FORCE
of
WORLD WAR TWO
in colour

Roger A. Freeman

BROCKHAMPTON PRESS
LONDON

Arms and Armour Press
An imprint of the Cassell Group
Wellington House,
125 Strand,
London WC2R 0BB

This edition published 1999 by Brockhampton Press,
a member of Hodder Headline PLC Group
ISBN 1 86019 8287

British Library Cataloguing-in-
Publication Data: a catalogue record
for this book is available from the
British Library

Edited and designed by Roger Chesneau
Typeset by Ronset Typesetters Ltd

Printed and bound in Dubai

Frontispiece Flt Lt W. H. Pentland, a No 417
Squadron pilot, entering the cockpit of
Spitfire V BR195/'AN-T'. (IWM)

Contents

Introducing Colour

Until the late 1940s colour photographs were, if not rare, a novelty in the United Kingdom and even then were usually only available as transparencies for projection or viewing with a magnifier. Their inclusion in printed works was limited by the high cost of the reproduction process. A number of techniques for producing colour photographs had been introduced during the early part of the century, but not until the launching of Kodachrome in the United States in 1935 was a truly viable colour product—viable in terms of process and of cost—marketed. From the commercially available 35mm stock, a limited amount had reached Britain prior to the outbreak of the Second World War. Also available in the immediate pre-war years was Dufaycolor, produced in England, and Agfa, from European sources.

Particularly where British forces are concerned, the photographic record of the 1939–45 war years is predominantly in black and white and comes from the work of official or accredited Press photographers. In fact, the use of private cameras on military installations was forbidden, although in some units this regulation was not strictly adhered to. Additionally, monochrome film gradually became scarce: by the mid-war years it was largely unobtainable by civilians.

Little colour photography of Royal Air Force subjects is known for the first year of hostilities, but in 1941 the Ministry of Information (MOI) arranged for the supply of some Kodachrome stock from the United States so that a collection of colour photographs could be made available for those few British publications that occasionally ran colour reproductions. Many of the original listings disappeared, but the residue of this transparency collection was passed to the Imperial War Museum after the war.

One supplier of colour transparencies to the MOI was Charles E. Brown, a freelance recognized pre-war as Britain's leading aerial photographer. Brown sold his monochrome work to several magazines but principally to *Aeronautics*. At that time none of the British aviation magazines had facilities for reproducing colour photographs. However, in the United States, by the late 1930s the most successful aviation magazine of the period, *Flying*, was regularly featuring a cover and often four inside pages in full colour. In 1941 arrangements were made by the Deputy Director of Public Relations, the Ministry of Information and the editor of *Flying*, Bill Ziff, for a special RAF issue of the magazine. This, from the British viewpoint, would boost the rather

Above A view of Bristol Beaufort 'S-Sugar' with its two Bristol Hercules radials warming up and the ground crew ready to pull away the wheel chocks at the pilot's signal. As No 217 Squadron often operated at night, the undersides of the aircraft were painted black. N1012 was SOC in May 1943. (IWM)

poor publicity their use of American-made aircraft was receiving in the United States. In November that year Ziff agreed to send 100 unexposed 5 × 4 Kodachrome transparencies to the UK for colour photographs, no material in this size being available in Britain. This resulted in two sets of 31 exposed transparencies being sent to the US the following May, one for use by *Flying* and the other to be retained by the British Information Service in Washington for its own use. The photographs of aircraft were mostly taken by Charles E. Brown, though there were also portraits by George Woodbine and a few shots were supplied by Fox Photos.

However, by various means, 35mm Kodachrome stock was already in the hands of a few British photographers. It appears that from early 1941 Charles Brown was carrying out some colour photography of RAF subjects on official Press Days at military airfields. He often carried two cameras, one loaded with black and white film and the other, a Zeiss Contact II, with the 35mm Kodachrome. He was usually sparing with the colour shots, sometimes taking only two or three during each event, although on rare occasions he appears to have exposed a whole reel (for example, during his visit to Waterbeach in the spring of 1942 to photograph Stirlings).

The British Services had their own photographers, predominantly men who had been professionally such during civilian life. Those in the RAF had access to a limited amount of Kodachrome from late 1942, and during the following year at least eight different photographers occasionally made use of colour, notably P Off W. Bellamy and Fg Off George Woodbine. It was Woodbine who took most of the colour photographs from West African and Mediterranean regions reproduced in this volume. RAF photographers sent much of their work to the MOI where, provided it passed the censor, the transparencies were made available for general publication. Colour photographs from the Far East were few and there appears to have been scant interest by the MOI in obtaining colour cover of all overseas military activities during 1944 and 1945. Where the RAF was concerned, most of the colour work in the UK continued to be done by Charles Brown who was, if anything, increasing his output in the final months of hostilities. His deal with *Flying* allowed Brown to amass the largest private collection of photographs of British aircraft and RAF subjects from the Second World War. This collection is now with the photographic library of the RAF Museum.

In addition to Fox, other British photographic agencies with access to colour were Sport and General, Keystone and Odhams Press. The results of Odhams' photography were published in its weekly magazine *Illustrated*; however, only a small proportion related to the RAF.

Unlike their British counterparts, US servicemen could obtain Kodachrome, usually sent by family members back home. Moreover, there was not such a severe prohibition on taking photographs at American military installations. In consequence, British aircraft that

Below left Wg Cdr John B. Selby, DSO, DFC, commanding No 23 Squadron (Mosquitos) on Malta, summer 1943. (IWM)

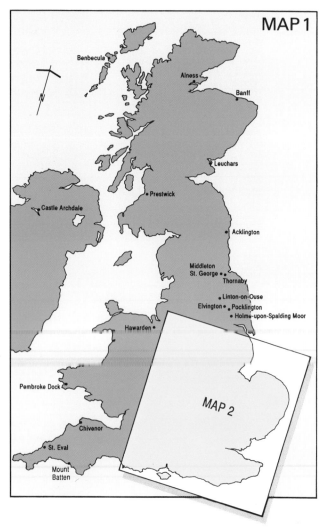

ABBREVIATIONS

AC	Aircraftman	Gp Capt	Group Captain	OTU	Operational Training Unit
ACM	Air Chief Marshal	HCU	Heavy Conversion Unit	PBY	US Navy designation for
AOC	Air Officer Commanding	HE	High-Explosive		aircraft type that also
AOC-in-C	Air Officer Commanding in	He	Heinkel		served in the RAF as the
	Chief	hp	horsepower		Catalina
ASR	Air/Sea Rescue (Services)	IAF	Indian Air Force	P Off	Pilot Officer
ATA	Air Transport Auxiliary	IWM	Imperial War Museum	PR	Photographic
B	Bomber	Ju	Junkers		Reconnaissance
CB	Companion of (the Order of)	KBE	Knight of the British Empire	RAF	Royal Air Force
	the Bath	KCB	Knight Commander of the	RAAF	Royal Australian Air Force
CMG	Companion of (the Order of)		Bath	RCAF	Royal Canadian Air Force
	St Michael and St George	KLM	*Koninklijke Luchtvaart*	SAAF	South African Air Force
CO	Commanding Officer		*Maatschappij* (Royal Dutch	SFTS	Service Flying Training
DC	Douglas Commercial		Airlines)		School
DFC	Distinguished Flying Cross	LAC	Leading Aircraftman	Sgt	Sergeant
DH	De Havilland	lb	pound (weight)	Sqn Ldr	Squadron Leader
DSO	Distinguished Service Order	LF	Low (Altitude) Fighter	SOC	Struck off charge
ECFS	Empire Central Flying School	LNER	London & North-Eastern	UK	United Kingdom
F	Fighter		Railway	US	United States
FB	Fighter Bomber	MC	Military Cross	USAAF	United States Army Air Force
Flt Lt	Flight Lieutenant	Me	Messerschmitt	VC	Victoria Cross
Fg Off	Flying Officer	MG	Morris Garages	VE-Day	Victory in Europe Day
Flt Sgt	Flight Sergeant	Mk	Mark	WAAF	Women's Auxiliary Air Force
ft	foot, feet	mm	millemetre(s)	Wg Cdr	Wing Commander
FTS	Flying Training School	MOI	Ministry of Information	WO	Warrant Officer
FW	Focke Wulf	mph	miles per hour		
		MU	Maintenance Unit		

Left and right Maps showing the locations of airfields mentioned in this book.

Left For long the mainstay of Bomber Command, the Vickers Wellington (or 'Wimpy' as it was popularly known) was a tried and trusty aircraft. Here a train of eighteen 250lb HE bombs is prepared for loading into a Wellington III of No 419 Squadron at Mildenhall on a cold January afternoon in 1942. (IWM)
Right Max Aitken's personal Mosquito FB.VI, serial HR366, code '01', ready to roll at Banff. On the strength of No 235 Squadron, it displays the red spinners of that unit. After the war this aircraft was sold to Turkey. (RAF Museum)

put down on USAAF airfields often engendered sufficient curiosity to warrant a camera pointed in their direction.

The following pages carry over 300 reproductions of the Second World War period that feature RAF- and Commonwealth air forces-related subjects. The majority come from the Imperial War Museum and RAF Museum collections and some may have appeared in other publications. Many result from Press Facility Days arranged by the Air Ministry's Public Relations Branch to allow the Press to feature certain aircraft types in service; hence colour photographs of a particular aircraft type tend to be concentrated on just one or two units. Much of the Charles Brown, agency and MOI material was taken in 1942 and 1943 when there was particular emphasis on the air war in Britain. In the final years of hostilities, newspaper and magazine photographers

ACKNOWLEDGEMENTS
A major problem encountered by the author in compiling this collection of colour photographs was the poor captions—if they existed—for those illustrations held by the Imperial War Museum and the RAF Museum. Wartime security forbade mention of units and locations and frequently the names of individuals, and to establish these identities half a century on was a difficult task requiring searches of records in several archives and much correspondence. In many cases, where a positive identification of subjects has been achieved it was often due to the expertise of acknowledged authorities on particular aspects of RAF history. For example, the captions for Lancaster aircraft and crews were compiled largely as a result of information supplied by Mike Garbett and Brian Goulding—who have spent very many years studying this most famous of British bombers—and associated mortals. Chris Thomas, the expert on Typhoon and Tempest aircraft and their pilots, was able to provide many details, while Philip Moyes dealt with Halifax and other bomber mysteries. The fact that locations have been identified owes much to Norman Ottaway and his perseverance and skill in scrutinizing maps and photographs for the vital clues. Bruce Robertson made his extensive knowledge of the Second World War RAF available and was of inestimable assistance in many areas. Others whose contributions are no less valued are: Wg Cdr H. Ambrose, Michael Bailey, Douglas Boards, Frank Cheesman, Ken Cothliff, Simon Clay, Jeff Ethell, David Dorrell, Bert Dowty, Douglas Fisher, Lee Gover, Ken Harbour, Alan Howorth, Merle Olmsted, Gen Reginald Lane, Air Vice-Marshal Michael Lyne, Roy Morris, Roy Nesbit, Paul Nisbet, John Rawlings, Wg Cdr C. L. C. Bob Roberts, Alastair Ross, F. E. Shute, Robert Sinclair, Ken Smy, Edgar Spridgeon and the Stirling Aircraft Association. The help given by the staffs at the Public Record Office at Kew, at the Imperial War Museum and at the RAF Museum is also appreciated, particularly the assistance rendered by Andrew Rennick, Paul Kemp, David Parry and Alan Williams. On the production side, Ian Mactaggart lent his photographic skills, Bruce Robertson gave editorial advice and Jean Freeman and Alice Apricot dealt diligently and decisively with providing the manuscript. To all I offer my most sincere thanks, and I hope that they will find this volume worthy of their contributions.

Despite extensive research, it has not been possible to name the individuals or locations depicted in some of the photographs in this volume. The author would therefore be pleased to hear from anyone who can make positive identifications. He would also be interested in the whereabouts of other colour photographs of RAF and Commonwealth air forces subjects taken in 1939–45.   **Roger A. Freeman**

were attracted elsewhere by the complexity of operations and the RAF did not receive so much of their attention.

The quality of photographs from other sources varies considerably, not helped by some 50 years' ageing. Several reproductions here are therefore not to present-day standards but are included because of the rarity of the colour images. In some cases the poor quality has been due to the photographer's unfamiliarity with the use of colour in setting his camera. Processing of the exposed film may also be a factor, where fading or tone changes are involved. Camouflage shades are the most affected in such circumstances but, in general, the colours are remarkably true to life.

The wartime captioning of officially accredited photographs was in most cases simplistic to the extreme and often failed to name individuals, to identify locations or to give dates, all in the cause of wartime security. In this volume every effort has been made to provide as much information as possible in identifying the subject and placing it in time to give a true historical perspective. If the lay reader sees no merit in the listing of aircraft serial numbers and unit identity markings, the explanation is that these are the keys to historical documentation. Aircraft markings are all indicative. An aircraft's serial number not only relates to the ordering of a particular contract batch but also provides a stable identity of the aircraft throughout its service history; code letters relate to the unit in which the aircraft was serving at the time of the photograph. Colours provide clues to an aircraft's intended role, and colour changes can reflect the progression from defence to offence. These facets have influenced the grouping of the photographs for presentation.

Pictures showing aircraft crewed and tended by smiling young men in a colourful setting may belie the underlying tragedies: a subject tracing has revealed that many of the individuals depicted were shortly to die and, similarly, many of the aircraft to be destroyed. The casualty rate in the wartime RAF was high and included many airmen from Canada, Australia, South Africa, New Zealand and the colonies who aligned themselves with Britain and joined the RAF, while others served in the air forces of their own Commonwealth countries.

Leading and Lesser Lights

Colour photography was generally viewed as a novelty by RAF personnel who came into contact with photographers whose cameras were loaded with Kodachrome, and having one's portrait captured in colour was an opportunity not likely to be turned down at a time when the majority had only ever known or encountered monotone photography. Many senior officers appear to have been willing subjects, and the resultant photographs were identified with their names; however, RAF wartime security decreed that other personnel, in most cases, remain anonymous, and this has left a legacy of unknown airmen and airwomen in much of the pictorial cover of the 1939–45 years.

Right Air Chief Marshal Sir Charles F. A. Portal, KCB, DSO, MC, Chief of the Air Staff 1940–45, about to enter a car outside Air Ministry buildings in London, July 1942. To all intents and purposes Portal was the 'boss man' of the RAF from 5 October 1940 until his retirement after the end of the war. Born on 21 May 1883, he became an RFC pilot in 1916 and was awarded the DSO and Bar and MC for his services on the Western Front. He died on 22 April 1971. (IWM)

Far right Air Chief Marshal Sir Arthur Tedder poses beside his four-star Jeep on the Italian coast, 17 December 1943. The affable, pipe-smoking Tedder returned to Britain that same month to take up his appointment as Deputy Commander of the Allied Expeditionary Forces then being assembled for the cross-Channel invasion. He died on 3 June 1967. (IWM)

Below right Air Chief Marshal Sir Arthur T. Harris, Commander-in-Chief Bomber Command from 22 February 1942 to 14 September 1945, was the most controversial of all RAF Commanders yet was probably the one most dedicated to his aims. He was affectionately known as 'Butch' by his men, who gave 55,573 of their lives—some 70 per cent of the total wartime RAF casualties (among wartime Commands, only the German U-Boat crews suffered a higher attrition rate of casualties). (IWM)

Right Air Marshal Sir Arthur S. Barratt, KCB, CMG, MC, in battledress and flying gear beside a Hurricane. He often flew this aircraft when visiting airfields of Army Co-operation Command, which he commanded at the date of this photograph in 1942. Barratt had commanded the RAF in France prior to the 1940 exodus, and he went on to head Technical Training Command. He was born on 25 February 1891 and he died on 4 November 1966. (IWM)

Far right, top Air Commodore Frank Whittle was the 'father of the jet engine', the prototype of which was bench-run in 1937. The models on his desk are of the first British prototype jet aircraft to fly and of the Meteor, the first jet to enter service with the RAF. (IWM)

Below right In sheepskin flying jacket and high-neck sweater, Air Vice-Marshal Sir Hugh Lloyd, KBE, CB, MC, DFC, stands beside the Beaufighter he flew to Britain on 18 March 1944; at the time he was AOC Mediterranean Allied Coastal Air Forces. His expertise in directing the air defence of Malta from May 1941 to August 1942 was acknowledged by the knighthood and earned him his next command. Later he was designated to command Tiger Force on Okinawa, which was to be the RAF contribution to the bombing of Japan. Born in 1895, he died in 1991. (IWM)

Far right, bottom Air Marshal Sir Arthur Coningham, Commander of the 2nd Tactical Air Force, discussing matters relating to Operation 'Varsity' (the crossing of the Rhine) with Field Marshal Sir Bernard Montgomery, commanding the 21st Army Group, and Lieutenant-General Sir Miles Dempsey, Commander of Britain's Second Army, in a German village on 22 March 1945. (IWM)

Left, top There were exceptions to the general policy of not identifying personnel depicted in photographs released for publication, particularly in the case of highly distinguished airmen. Wg Cdr Guy Gibson, of 'dam-busting' fame, was one, and when Fg Off George Woodbine visited Scampton on 22 July 1943 to take a series of publicity pictures the renowned bomber pilot co-operated in this notable pose. Poppies growing on an earth blast-bank make a striking backdrop. (IWM)

Left, bottom In contrast to the previous photograph, this portrait, taken later the same year, was issued with the simple caption 'A Royal Air Force bomber pilot'. A half-century later, it was identified by the subject and his wife: he is Flt Lt Douglas Alaric Boards, serving *circa* October 1943 as Captain of No 15 Squadron Stirling EH930 'LS-A' at Mildenhall. He completed 23 raids and later flew another five with No 635 Squadron, a pathfinder unit, at Downham Market. (IWM)

Right, top Another portrait of 'A Royal Air Force bomber pilot', issued at the same time as that of Flt Lt Boards and presumably also depicting a No 15 Squadron airman. (IWM)

Far right, top 'Bomber airmen studying a map before a raid' was the extent of the original caption of this 1941 photograph of a somewhat hackneyed pose for air crew in flying clothes. Not even the aircraft type the airmen flew was mentioned. (IWM)

Right, bottom In some instances the photographers recorded the name of officers but rarely those of other ranks. While George Woodbine's notes identified this pilot as Flt Lt Pentland, the members of the No 417 Squadron ground crew remained anonymous. Fortunately, a more relaxed attitude towards the publicity of individuals existed during the final months of hostilities. (IWM)

Far right, bottom Enemy action and flying accidents severely restricted the chances of any operational RAF pilot of 1939 surviving until 1945. Fate was unusually kind to some, although in the case of Frank Griffiths his skills undoubtedly aided his survival of a number of serious incidents. He joined the RAF in 1936 and served for 41 years, a quarter of his service being with research and development units. In August 1943 he was shot down in eastern France while on a supply-dropping mission to the Maquis and was the only survivor of his Halifax crew. Evading capture, he spent the next three months escaping from enemy-held territory and returning to Britain. This photograph of Frank Griffiths, then a Flight Lieutenant, was taken in January 1943 when he was with the Telecommunications Flying Unit. The aircraft is Walrus L2201. (Douglas Fisher)

LEADING AND LESSER LIGHTS

Bombing in Black

Victory in the Second World War was achieved partly by the weakening of Germany by Allied bombing. While the Americans bombed by day, the RAF operated by night, so that for the concealment of the latter's bombers the predominant camouflage colour was black. In stating this, it is of course realized that black is not really a colour at all: colours are seen by light reflection, and total darkness is thus not a colour. But this is just what the black of bombers was for—a sooty, non-reflecting, anti-searchlight black. For concealment from the air when dispersed on airfields, all RAF operational aircraft types were on production given a camouflage in a disruptive pattern of Dark Earth (brown) and Dark Green covering the upper surfaces and sides. The colour of the under surfaces depended on the role: for bombers like the Whitley and Wellington it was black, while for the smaller bombers like the Blenheim (which were expected to operate by day) it was Sky, a pale blue/grey. Initially the night bombers were expected occasionally to operate by day, but prohibitive losses forced them into a purely night role. In consequence their black undersurfaces were extended halfway up the fuselage sides and in 1941 the black was extended still further so that only the strict plan view remained in brown and green. After the war in Europe there came about a reversal in the extremes of the colour range for the aircraft of Tiger Force forming up to take the war to Japan from a Pacific base: just the under surfaces remained in black, the upper and side surfaces being in heat-reflecting white.

Right, top During the first two years of hostilities the RAF's main light bomber force operating from the British mainland consisted of an average of eight squadrons of Bristol Blenheims under the control of No 2 Group based in East Anglia. Here members of the air and ground crews of No 21 Squadron, which flew the Blenheim IV for a longer period than any other squadron in the Group, pose with one of their aircraft at Watton on 18 August 1941. (L. Gover)

Right, bottom Back at Watton after a successful attack on shipping off the Dutch coast, the No 21 Squadron gunner of Blenheim IV V6436/'YH-L' (believed to be Fg Off Albert Collins) climbs from his hatch, having given parachute and harness to a member of the ground staff, 18 August 1941. The Blenheim was too slow and its main defensive armament, of two .303 machine guns in the dorsal power turret, too light to give it much chance of surviving a determined interception by its main antagonist, the Messerschmitt Bf 109. Ten days later V6436, with P Off Frank Orme, P Off Stanley Gunnis amd Fg Off Collins, was one of seven from a force of eighteen Blenheims lost in an attack on Rotterdam. (Hulton)

Left, top and bottom The longest-ranged of the Command's bombers at the outbreak of war was the plodding Whitley. It operated almost exclusively in darkness with No 4 Group, which had six squadrons in the York area. Fully loaded, the Whitley was hard-pressed to reach and maintain 12,000ft, making it vulnerable to enemy ground defences. The crew seen watching engine adjustments to Z6743 at Middleton St George, Durham, are members of No 78 Squadron. The aircraft being serviced, Z6577/'EY-F', was one of seven Whitleys from a force of 29 that failed to return from an attempt to bomb rail targets at Cologne some six weeks later, on the night of 16/17 August 1941. (IWM)

Right, top The Whitley had a pronounced tail-up 'sit' in flight. These two aircraft parading for the camera were soon to come back to earth for the last time: 'EY-V' (serial number Z6743) was abandoned by the crew near Ipswich on the return from a raid on Düsseldorf on 25 August 1941 and crash-landed itself at Mistley, Essex; 'EY-L' (Z6625) crash-landed near Bircham Newton on 9 July 1941, a few days after this photograph was taken. (Hulton)

Right, centre The ungainly looking Hampden medium bomber equipped six operational and two reserve squadrons of No 5 Group in the Grantham area when hostilities began; at peak inventory in 1941 the Group had ten squadrons and some 150 Hampdens. X2898/'OL-N', seen in the photograph running up its engines at Scampton in the winter of 1941–42, was one of the many Hampdens that were modified for torpedo-carrying duties when the type was withdrawn from service with Bomber Command. This particular machine was lost serving with No 415 Squadron RCAF on 19 August 1943. (Hulton)

Right, bottom Ready to go: the Canadian pilot of a Wellington obliges the photographer by sticking his head out of the small cockpit window. (IWM)

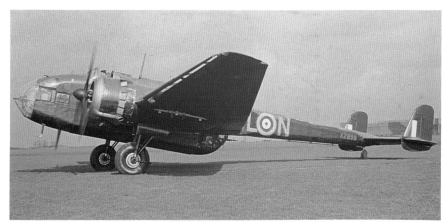

Left, top Wellington III Z1572, seen flying ENE some three miles east of Thetford (the road is that from Brettenham to Bridgham) on 27 May 1942 when serving with No 419 Squadron. This unit was the third Canadian-crewed bomber squadron to be formed in the UK. Z1572 served first with Nos 115 and 75 Squadrons and went on to fly for another RCAF squadron, No 427, before being pensioned off for training duties with No 16 OTU. The bomber was finally SOC on 30 April 1945. (RAF Museum)

Left, centre Ground crew push a 4,000lb blast bomb towards the bay of a No 419 Squadron Wellington at Mildenhall, 27 May 1942. This weapon was known as a 'Cookie'. (IWM)

Left, bottom The first of the four-engine heavy bombers to enter service, the Short Stirling eventually equipped seven squadrons in No 3 Group at airfields in the Cambridge–Huntingdon area. The first, No 7, started to receive Stirlings in August 1940 and this unit took the new bomber for its first operation on the night of 10/11 February 1941, an attack on oil storage tanks at Rotterdam. Here a No 7 Squadron crew wait to enter battered Stirling I W7446/'MG-S', during a Press Day at Oakington in October 1941. Like many Stirlings, W7446 was wrecked in a landing accident when, on 18 November 1941, it swung on touch-down, causing the undercarriage to collapse. (S. Clay)

Right, top Wellington B.X HE575 never flew in anger. Manufactured by Vickers-Armstrong at Hawarden early in 1943, this aircraft served in operational training units for eighteen months before being used as a static instructional airframe. When photographed in the summer of 1944 it was serving as 'Y7-J' with No 86 OTU, which only existed for four months (15 June–15 October 1944) at Gamston. (Air Force Academy)

Right, bottom A seven-man crew from No 149 Squadron under the towering nose of a Stirling at Mildenhall, Suffolk, on the chill 16 January 1942. The aircraft, W7455/'OJ-B', survived combat operations with this unit and two other squadrons, only to be shot down by an enemy night intruder into a cornfield at Great Thurlow while serving with No 1657 Heavy Conversion Unit. (IWM)

Right, top Manpower was not the usual or desirable method for moving a 25-ton Stirling on the ground, but the scene makes a good subject for the photographer. The long, double-folding retraction arrangement of the Stirling's undercarriage was prone to failure: this aircraft, W7462/'OJ-T', suffered an undercarriage collapse when landing on 29 January 1942. (S. Clay)

Right, bottom, and far right, top Good weather on Press Facility Day, 29 April 1942, at Waterbeach, Cambridgeshire, provided Charles Brown with an opportunity to take several colour photographs of No 1651 Heavy Conversion Unit which, as the name implies, served to make bomber crews trained on one type competent to handle another. Here Stirling N6101, one of the first built by Short & Harland at Belfast, towers above a bomb train of sixteen 250-pounders. While a Stirling could accommodate as many as twenty-four 500lb bombs and deliver them at short range, its bay could not house the large bombs that the Lancaster's could accept. (IWM)

Far right, bottom Mechanics busy on the engines of a No 1651 HCU Stirling. (RAF Museum)

Far left, top Refuelling at Waterbeach. A Stirling had seven tanks in each wing and a total capacity of 2,254 Imperial gallons—sufficient to allow a 5,000lb bomb load to be flown 900 miles from base in favourable weather conditions. (RAF Museum)

Far left, bottom Sgt Leonard A. Johnson and crew walking beneath the nose of Stirling N3676/'S' of 1651 HCU at Waterbeach while the ground crew run up the engines. The four Bristol Hercules X radials developed sufficient power to speed this large and heavy aircraft at around 200mph at operational altitude. (IWM)

Left, top Last-minute instructions for Sgt Leonard Johnson and crew prior to a flight in N3676. Left to right in this posed shot are believed to be Sgt J. King (navigator), Sqn Ldr Granger, Sgt. L. A. Johnson (pilot), Sgt Rennie (engineer), Sgt Lofthouse (W Op), Sgt Jock McGown (rear gunner) and Sgt Agg. This crew joined No 214 Squadron in May 1942 and on their sixth operation their Stirling was badly damaged by enemy aircraft. The crew were ordered to bail out but Johnson was able to regain control although the navigator had already jumped. 'Johnny' Johnson was a Texan, and after completing a tour he joined the US Navy, only to be lost in a PBY flying boat accident. (RAF Museum)

Left, bottom Sgt Jock McGown in the rear turret of Stirling N3676 at Waterbeach. He was to prove adept at handling this position, for later, when the crew was with No 214 Squadron, he was credited with sharing in the destruction of one Bf 110 night fighter on 29 July 1942 and another on 28 August 1942, and with damaging a similar aircraft on 15 August that year. (RAF Museum)

Left, top A flight of No 1651 HCU Stirlings flying NNW over Little Thetford, Cambridgeshire, 29 April 1942. All these aircraft eventually came to grief. Aircraft 'G' (N6096) only served with No 1651 HCU and was lost on the Hamburg raid of 29 July 1942; 'S' (N3676), with previous service in No 15 Squadron, crashed on take-off at Waterbeach on 30 July 1942; and 'C' (N6069) also flew with No 15 Squadron and endured with 1651 HCU until take-off on 20 April 1943 when its pilots lost control and the aircraft crashed. (RAF Museum)

Left, bottom Another view of three Stirlings from No 1651 HCU flying south-west, with the outskirts of Waterbeach in the left foreground and Cambridge in the distance. The Stirling was the only one of the three RAF wartime four-engine heavy bombers that was designed as such from the outset. Although it was a good, stable aircraft in flight and surprisingly manoeuvrable, its weight was supported by a wing of short span owing to the design requirement that the aircraft could be housed in the standard pre-war hangars which had 100ft door openings. The wing area was the chief limiting factor in the Stirling's poor operational altitude when loaded. To shorten take-offs and landings, a very high main undercarriage was fitted to give the wing a sufficient angle of incidence to promote good lift. This made take-offs and landings tricky with the Stirling, which had a tendency to swing violently unless carefully handled. (RAF Museum)

Right, top In this view the Stirlings are south of Over and just west of Oakington. (RAF Museum)

Right, bottom Stirlings of No 90 Squadron lined up on the perimeter track at Wratting Common on 31 August 1943; the crews are awaiting take-off time. The target was Berlin, and of the 622 bombers dispatched by Bomber Command that night 106 were Stirlings, of which seventeen were lost (mostly shot down by night fighters); No 90 Squadron lost one of its nineteen Stirlings operating. Stirlings were only sent to Berlin on one more occasion as they were too vulnerable to the defences. (IWM)

Left, top The Handley Page Halifax was the second of the four-engine heavy bombers to enter service. The first squadron to be equipped was No 35, which commenced operations with the type on the night of 11/12 March 1941. The Halifax had its share of problems, not the least of which was a propensity to go into an uncontrollable spin if stalled. This is Halifax B.II Series I W7676/'TL-P', being flown by Flt Lt Reginald Lane and crew and photographed near Linton-on-Ouse in late June 1942. Flt Lt Lane and crew flew twelve operations in this aircraft, and Reg Lane went on to distinguish himself in No 6 Group RCAF, retiring from the Canadian armed services as a Lieutenant-General. W7676 failed to return from an operation against Nuremberg on the night of 28/29 August 1942 with Flt Sgt D. A. John and crew. (RAF Museum)

Left, bottom W7676/'TL-P' flying with W7749 'TL-F'. The latter, which was usually flown by P Off K. Reynolds and crew, survived operations and in March 1943 was retired to No 1659 HCU, but it was wrecked in a crash on 2 August 1944. (RAF Museum)

Right, top Mechanics at work on the Merlin engines of a Halifax II of No 35 Squadron at Linton-on-Ouse, June 1942. The Merlin X-model engines, rated at 1,075hp for take-off, were found to provide insufficient power for combat operations. (IWM)

Right, centre A Halifax of No 102 Squadron nicknamed *Ye Olde Black Bitch*, with 22 raid symbols, is signalled to its dispersal point at Pocklington in early February 1943. (IWM)

Right, bottom A Halifax II Series I (Special) of No 77 Squadron taking off from Polebrook on 30 May 1943. This aircraft has the nose turret and other external equipment judged extraneous removed as part of an effort to improve performance. There were many mystifying crashes involving Halifaxes getting into uncontrolled dives. After many months this problem was finally attributed to rudder stalling—in some conditions the rudder became locked over hard. As a result, the original triangular-shape tailfins were replaced by a more rectangular design, which helped to overcome the difficulty. (USAAF)

Left, top While a rigger cleans the cockpit perspex, an armourer rods the barrels of the front turrets of a recently received Halifax I at Linton-on-Ouse. (IWM)

Left, bottom The first RCAF bomber squadron to be formed overseas was No 405 in April 1941, at first with Wellingtons but converting to Halifaxes a year later. In front of this Halifax II at the Squadron's Topcliffe base on a bright September day in 1942 are bomb trolleys carrying the ownership mark '405'. These apparently escaped the wartime censor's notice when this picture was approved for publication. (Hulton)

Above Sgt T. Todd, the rear gunner of Sgt H. V. Gawler's crew on Halifax JB811/'KN-J', looks over his guns as the aircraft prepares to take off from Polebrook. Five aircraft of No 77 Squadron were diverted to this airfield after operations on the night of 29/30 May 1943. (USAAF)

Right, top A crew entering Manchester L7483 of No 207 Squadron on 11 November 1941 at Waddington. The Manchester, basically the twin-engine forerunner of the Lancaster, was continually plagued with engine trouble, its underdeveloped 1,760hp Vultures being prone to fail under prolonged full power. (Via S. Clay)

Right, centre L7483, nicknamed *Hobson's Choice*, flew but four raids in six months—an indication of the engine problems which beset the Manchester and led to periods of grounding. This particular aircraft eventually became a static instructional airframe. (Hulton)

Right, bottom Three Avro Lancaster Is of No 207 Squadron, a unit which began converting to this most successful of the three RAF heavies in March 1942 while based at Bottisford. Of the aircraft depicted, L7583/'EM-A' and L7580/'EM-C' survived combat operations, were retired to non-combat units and saw out the war. R5570/'EM-F', however, was less fortunate: captained by No 207's CO, Wg Cdr F. G. L. Bain, it was the only Lancaster lost of 108 attacking Turin on the night of 8/9 December 1942. This photograph was taken by Charles Brown on 20 June 1942. (RAF Museum)

Left, top Work on the port engines of a Lancaster, believed to be a No 207 Squadron aircraft near the technical site at Bottesford in June 1942. The thick lines painted on the wings are walkway guides. (IWM)

Left, bottom Another view from the cockpit of the same Lancaster, showing activity around the starboard Merlins. (IWM)

Right, top During the war the most widely published photographs of a Lancaster in flight were those featuring R5689/'VN-N' of No 50 Squadron which, in the hands of Sqn Ldr Hugh Everitt, performed for cameramen on 28 August 1942, flying from Swinderby. It was wrecked three weeks later, on the night of 18/19 September, in a crash at Thurlby while returning from a sea mining operation. Four of the crew were killed and three injured. However, this Lancaster's image would appear frequently in publications for many years to come. (Via S. Clay)

Right, centre A view from the top of a bomb dump blast mound at Swinderby, 28 August 1942, the day Lancaster R5689/'VN-N' demonstrated in the Lincolnshire skies for photographers. The subject is parked on the perimeter track and beyond is No 50 Squadron's dispersal area, looking west. (MOI)

Right, bottom Testing the tyre pressure of Lancaster R5540 of No 44 Squadron Conversion Flight at Waddington on 29 September 1942. (IWM)

Right, top Precarious work: held by another mechanic for safety, a fitter is engrossed in remedial repairs to the mid upper turret of R5540. (IWM)

Right, bottom A gunner—believed to be Sgt J. Bell—looks through the opening in the perspex of the rear turret of R5740/'KM-O'. The four .303 Browning machine guns could discharge at a combined rate of 7,000 rounds a minute but were outranged by the heavy-calibre cannon of most *Luftwaffe* night fighters. (IWM)

Far right, top A rigger touches up the code letters 'KM-Ō'. Until June 1942 these squadron and plane-in-squadron letters had been light grey, but dull red was then substituted because it was less conspicuous in moonlight. The bar above the individual letter indicated the second 'O-Orange' in a squadron and exemplifies what became general practice, but in this case it also distinguished No 44 Squadron's Conversion Flight. R5540 was written off in a crash-landing at Winthorpe the following January while serving with No 1661 HCU. (IWM)

Far right, bottom The seven men of a Lancaster wait near the crew room at Waddington for transport out to their aircraft. (IWM)

Left, top Rod-cleaning the front machine guns of Lancaster R5666/'KM-F'; another member of the ground crew is cleaning the cockpit windows (night flying presented enough visibility problems without dirt on the perspex!). This Lancaster was usually flown by WO Frank Stott and crew. They completed their tour, but R5666 failed to return from Nienburg while being flown by another crew on 17/18 December 1942. (IWM)

Left, bottom Lancaster R5740/'KM-O' taxies out at Waddington for air-to-air photography on 29 September 1942; at the controls is Sqn Ldr 'Pat' Burnett, the 'B' Flight commander. Delivered to No 44 Squadron in July 1942, R5740 endured for nearly a year until going missing on the night of 25/26 June 1943. (IWM)

Right, top Canadian P Off A. S. Jess, wireless operator of Sqn Ldr Burnett's crew, carrying two pigeon boxes. Homing pigeons served as a means of communication in the event of a crash, ditching or radio failure. They were registered by ring number, colour and sex, and their records had a remarks column! Waddington's C-type hangars can be seen in the background. (IWM)

Far right, top The motif on Lancaster I, W4118/'ZN-Y' of No 106 Squadron at Syerston, early November 1942. *Admiral Prune* was often used by Wg Cdr Guy Gibson, the squadron CO, or his 'B' Flight commander, Sqn Ldr John 'Dim' Wooldridge; the smiling face in the cockpit is that of P Off Jimmy Cooper. The white bomb symbol generally indicated a daylight raid. Because the Squadron often dropped sea mines (known as 'Gardening') and at the time naval officers were attached to the unit, it took a nautical stance with several of the aircraft displaying 'Admiral'-prefixed nicknames. *Admiral Prune* flew 640 hours before being lost on the Turin raid of 4/5 February 1943. (MOI)

Right, bottom Seen here on an air test in January 1943, Lancaster ED592 was delivered to No 50 Squadron on 7 February 1943. Its operational life was short—seven raids—for it fell at Zoelen, in the Netherlands, on the night of 1/2 March 1943. This photograph is an outstanding example of Charles Brown's love of a dramatic cloud background for his subjects. (RAF Museum)

Left, top Lancasters of No 50 Squadron up from Skellingthorpe in a spread formation on 26 August 1943. The two bombers beyond the wing tip are 'VN-D' and 'VN-J'. The former, serial number JA899, was missing on the night of 24/25 June 1944 with P Off L. G. Peters and crew. (IWM)

Left, centre A pilot's view over the two starboard Merlins from the cockpit of a No 50 Squadron Lancaster on 26 August 1943. (IWM)

Left, bottom On 27 May 1943 HM King George VI visited Scampton to make awards to members of No 617 Squadron for their epic 'dam-busting' raid on 16/17 May 1943. Here Wg Cdr Guy Gibson, who was awarded the Victoria Cross four days earlier, parades with members of his squadron. In the front row are Gibson's flight commanders, on his right Sqn Ldr 'Dave' Maltby and on his left Sqn Ldr 'Mick' Martin (who, after the war, became Air Marshal Sir Harold Martin, KCB, DSO*, DFC*, AFC). (IWM)

Right, top The King talks to Gibson while high-ranking RAF officers wait nearby. The Lancaster in the background bearing a wing commander's pennant on the fuselage is that of No 57 Squadron's CO, Wg Cdr Hopcroft. (IWM)

Right, centre The King has a word with Flt Lt H. S. Wilson. Air Vice-Marshal Ralph Cochrane, Commander of No 5 Group, is in the centre background and Guy Gibson is in the right foreground. (IWM)

Far right, centre The King talks to Flt Lt Les Munro from New Zealand. Gibson is on the right and Cochrane is behind Munro and to the right. (IWM)

Right, bottom The King inspects a line-up of ground crewmen beneath the nose of a Lancaster. *Frederick* III, ED989/'DX-F', has a motif derived from a caricature of Wg Cdr 'Freddie' Campbell Hopcroft, CO of No 57 Squadron, which shared Scampton with No 617 Squadron at this date. This Lancaster was one of 23 lost on the Peenemünde raid of 17/18 August 1943 when skippered by Wg Cdr W. R. Haskell, No 57 Squadron's new CO. A total of 597 Bomber Command aircraft operated that night, of which 324 were Lancasters. The far Lancaster in the photograph is Wg Cdr Guy Gibson's 'AJ-G'. (IWM)

Left, top Guy Gibson, answering a photo-call at Scampton, is seen here at his desk with Sqn Ldr D. J. H. 'Dave' Maltby, one of his flight commanders, on 22 July 1943. (IWM)

Left, bottom Flt Lt Dave Shannon, pilot of ED929/'AJ-L' on the dams raid, with Flt Lt R. D. Trevor-Roper (who flew as Gibson's rear gunner on the dams raid) and Sqn Ldr G. W. Holden at Scampton on 22 July 1943. (IWM)

Right, top The crew of Lancaster ED825/ 'AJ-T' on the dams raid pose under stormy clouds. Left to right are P Off D. A. MacLean (navigator), Flt Lt J. C. McCarthy (pilot) and Sgt L. Eaton (gunner); in the rear are Sgt R. Batson (gunner) and Sgt W. G. Ratcliffe (engineer). (IWM)

Right, centre Flt Lt H. S. Wilson's crew. Left to right are Flt Sgt T. H. Payne (gunner), P Off T. W. Johnson (engineer), Flt Sgt W. E. Hornby (rear gunner), Sgt L. G. Mieyette (w/op), P Off G. H. Coles (bomb-aimer) Fg Off J. A. Rodger (navigator) and Flt Lt Wilson. All were killed when their Lancaster was shot down on the night of 15/16 September 1943 during the disastrous raid mounted against the Dortmund–Ems Canal. (IWM)

Right, bottom The Soviet leader, not yet universally vilified, provided a patriotic nickname for aircraft 'J' of No 101 Squadron, serial number ED382, purportedly photographed on 4 May 1943 at Holme-on-Spalding Moor with twenty raids to its credit. The usual crew at this time was that of Fg Off Don Austin. The bomber proved as tough as its namesake, for it went on to serve with two other squadrons—Nos 625 and 300—plus a number of training units, to end as an instructional airframe after the war. (Via S. Clay)

Left, top The King and Queen inspect flight and ground crews on a visit to Warboys, a station of No 8 Pathfinder Group, on 10 February 1944. A No 156 Squadron Lancaster is seen in a T2 hangar. (IWM)

Left, bottom A gathering of No 467 Squadron men to celebrate the completion of 100 operations by Lancaster R5868/'PO-S' after its sortie on 11/12 May 1944 to a communications target in Belgium. The bomber started operations on 8/9 July 1942 with No 83 Squadron (where it was 'OL-Q') and reputedly flew 79 trips from Wyton and Scampton until being withdrawn for a major overhaul in August 1943. It joined No 467 Squadron RAAF at Waddington in November 1943 and went on to a reputed 137 sorties, the last on 23 April 1945 to Flensburg. Records indicate that the official 100th operation was not, strictly speaking, the actual one. This aircraft is now often photographed in colour, preserved as it is at the RAF Museum, Hendon. (IWM)

Right, top The night's load—a 4,000lb 'Cookie' and incendiary clusters—is delivered to a No 101 Squadron Lancaster at Holme-on-Spalding Moor, 4 May 1943. (Via S. Clay)

Right, centre Lancaster LM644/'HW-B' in the freezing conditions of Christmas Day 1944, one of ten No 100 Squadron aircraft diverted to Bungay after a raid on Cologne the previous evening. The yellow disc on the nose is a gas detection patch, common to all No 1 Group aircraft at this time. (A. Krassman)

Right, bottom The De Havilland Mosquito was renowned for its speed and bomb load relative to its size. The bomber version, the Mk IV, entered service in the summer of 1942. This example, DK338, is seen during a test flight from Hatfield in September that year and was later delivered to 105 Squadron at Marham. It served with that unit until crashing on its approach to the airfield on 1 May 1943. (RAF Museum)

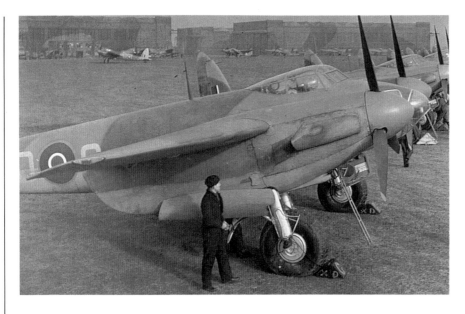

Left, top A line of Mosquito B.IVs of No 139 Squadron, the second unit armed with the bomber version, displayed for the Press. Marham's C-type hangars are prominent in the background. Nearest the camera is DZ421/'XD-G', the CO's (Wg Cdr Shand's) aircraft, which survived many hours of operational flying but broke up in the air over Acklam, Yorkshire, on 25 July 1944 when serving with No 1655 Mosquito Training Unit. (MOI)

Left, centre Set up for photographers here is a load of 500lb HE bombs, of which the Mosquito's bay could accommodate four. The No 139 Squadron 'scotty' mascot matches the spinners of DZ476/'XD-S', which was usually flown by Fg Off G. S. W. Rennie and P Off W. Embrey. (MOI)

Left, bottom Mosquitos of No 139 Squadron in echelon, February 1943. The aircraft nearest the camera, DZ373/'XD-B', was the only aircraft lost of the twelve that attacked the Liège armament works on 12 March 1943. It came down in the Scheldt. The pilot was Sgt R. M. Pace and the navigator P Off G. Cook. (MOI)

Right, top The Mosquito B.XVI had bulged bomb-bay doors to allow a 4,000lb HE blast bomb to be carried. ML963 '8K-K' was used by No 571 Squadron, a unit specially formed in April 1944 to increase the strength of the so-called Light Night Striking Force of No 8 Pathfinder Group, which engaged chiefly in high-level attacks with 'Cookies' (4,000lb bombs) against German industrial centres to maintain continual disruption. ML963 was missing in action, the only Mosquito failing to return from a force of 170 sent to Berlin on the night of 11/12 April 1945. The photograph was taken on 30 September 1944 when ML963 was flying from Oakington. (RAF Museum)

Right, bottom Of the several types of American-made light and medium bombers used by the RAF, the most redoubtable was the North American Mitchell. It was used operationally by only five RAF squadrons, but several of the aircraft endured for nearly three years. One of the first Mitchell squadrons was No 180, which took the type into action on 22 January 1943. This line-up at Foulsham for the Mitchell's introduction to the Press on 28 July 1943 depicts FL684 'EV-S' in the foreground, which survived the war; FL707/'EV-Z', the next in line, later went to No 98 Squadron and crashed at East Dereham after hitting high-tension cables. (RAF Museum)

Left, top *Nulli Secundus* was Mitchell FL218/'EV-W', which flew several missions, finally having to crash-land at Hawkinge on 25 January 1944 after suffering flak damage. FL685/'EV-B' was shot down by flak at Bunnières on 28 March 1944. (RAF Museum)

Left, centre Mitchell 'EV-P' being taken apart by a repair and salvage unit for use as spares, Melsbroek, Belgium, January 1945. (RAF Museum)

Left, bottom Even in wartime there was an opportunity for sailing enthusiasts to indulge their passion on the Norfolk Broads. The yachts were an enticement for low-level passes by pilots of both the RAF and USAAF. Here a Swanton Morley Mitchell skims over the sails on a bright summer afternoon in 1944. (J. Seward)

Right, top Another stalwart from a US production line was the Douglas Boston, first used operationally as a light bomber by No 88 Squadron in October 1941. Two of its Boston IIIs were photographed over Docking, Norfolk (Docking airfield can be seen to the left of the Docking–Burnham Market road) when a Press Day was held at Attlebridge on 21 May 1942. At the time the identification letters were being changed from Sky to red, in compliance with an Air Ministry requirement to make them less conspicuous if night operations were undertaken. No 88 retained the Boston until the unit disbanded on the Continent in April 1945. (Hulton)

Right, bottom Armourers clean and inspect the port nose package guns of Boston III AL693/'RH-U' at Attlebridge on 21 May 1942. This aircraft served with No 88 Squadron for several months and after overhaul was sent to the Mediterranean war zone, where it was destroyed in a force landing at Ckicherunti, Sicily, on 17 September 1943 while serving with No 114 Squadron. (Hulton)

Fighting Colours

Like bombers, fighters in production from 1937 had Dark Earth (brown) and Dark Green upper and side surfaces, but with Sky under surfaces in the Temperate Land Scheme camouflage. For a period at the beginning of the war, in order to aid aircraft identification for newly called-up Territorial anti-aircraft gunners and searchlight crews, the port wing under surfaces were painted black, but by the time of the Battle of Britain this virtually black/white display had been discontinued.

From late 1940 a 'tip and tail' identification feature, in addition to the national identity roundels, was introduced to assist recognition for pilots in fighting evolutions. This took the form of Sky-painted propeller spinners and an 18in band in the same colour around the rear fuselage.

Perhaps the most significant change to fighters based in Britain came in August 1941 when the two-tone camouflage colours were altered to Dark Green and Ocean Grey (with under surfaces now in Medium Sea Grey). This reflected the change from defence to offence as fighters swept over the Channel to force the *Luftwaffe* into retaining a strong fighter force in France and the Low Countries—means of drawing off pressure from the Russian Front.

Towards the end of the war, with air superiority assured on all fronts, some fighters were delivered in a highly polished natural metal finish to overcome the drag imposed by matt camouflage paints.

Right, top One of the earliest known air-to-air wartime photographs of RAF aircraft was taken by Fg Off M. D. Lyne of No 19 Squadron while patrolling over the Channel in the spring of 1940. The pilot of Spitfire I 'QV-K' was Sqn Ldr Geoffrey Stevenson and that of 'QV-O' Fg Off Watson. Both men were shot down near Dunkirk on 26 May 1940; Stevenson became a prisoner-of-war but Watson was killed. (AVM M. D. Lyne)
Right, bottom Spitfire II P7895, flying from Acklington with Flt Lt R. Deacon Elliott at the controls, over the coast in April 1941. The aircraft sports the code letters 'RN' that identified No 72 Squadron. It had previously served with No 65 Squadron and later it joined No 74 Squadron before being retired to training duties with Nos 57 and 53 OTUs. Its demise came during a take-off from Peterborough on 8 March 1945 while in use by No 7 SFTS.

Left, top Some idea of the attrition among fighter pilots in the early years of hostilities can be gained from the individual fates of this No 19 Squadron gathering outside Fowlmere's Nissen huts early in 1941. Second from the right is Sqn Ldr Brian Lane, CO from September 1940 until July 1941: he was killed the following December. On the extreme right is P Off A. F. Vokes, who was killed on 5 September 1942. Fourth from the left, facing the camera, is Fg Off W. J. 'Farmer' Lawson, who by July 1941 had been elevated to Squadron Leader and CO of No 19, only to lose his life on 28 August that year. (AVM M. D. Lyne)

Left, centre Refuelling a Spitfire II at an Operational Training Unit. The Spitfire's fuel supply came from two tanks totalling 85 Imperial gallons, located between the rear of the engine and the cockpit firewall, and a bowser needed about five minutes to fill them. The location of the tanks made the cockpit an unhealthy place to be if the fuel was ignited. (IWM)

Left, bottom Ground crew members adjusting the straps for Flt Lt Laurie in Spitfire V *Flying Scotsman* (BM202/'ZD-H') of No 222 Squadron. This was the second aircraft bearing this name to be paid for from donations made by LNER personnel, arranged through the company's wartime headquarters at Hitchin, a station through which the famous passenger train passed on its way north. (RAF Museum)

Right, top *Flying Scotsman*'s 1,470hp Merlin 45 bursts into life, belching flame from the exhaust stacks at North Weald, 4 May 1942. Later in the day this aircraft took part in a sweep over Gravelines. (IWM)

Right, bottom Warming up, BM202/'ZD-H' prepares to taxi out. The individual aircraft letter of this No 222 Squadron aircraft is carried under the nose as well as in the normal positions on the fuselage sides. Red tapes over the eight machine gun ports prevent the ingress of dirt. *Flying Scotsman* later went to No 242 Squadron and was SOC in June 1943. (IWM)

Left, top Sqn Ldr R. M. Milne's Spitfire V AD233/'ZD-F', of No 222 Squadron, flying north-west towards Dunmow, Essex, on 4 May 1942. Below, on the right, is Plesheybury and above the aircraft are Acreland Green and Stagden Cross. Three weeks later, on 25 May 1942, this aircraft would be shot down by FW 190s over Ostend while being flown by Sqn Ldr J. Jankiewicz, who was leading the Squadron. The Spitfire V was a poor match for the *Luftwaffe* fighter. (RAF Museum)

Left, bottom On 6 August 1943 Charles Brown took air-to-air photographs of a 'clipped-wing' Spitfire LF.V, BL479/'SZ-X' of the Polish-manned No 316 ('City of Warsaw') Squadron. This unit, based at Northolt, was at the time in the process of converting from Spitfire IXs to LF.Vs for low-altitude operations. (RAF Museum)

Right, top A contrast in size: a Spitfire V of No 402 Squadron, RCAF, based at Digby, flying in formation with a P-47C Thunderbolt of the 84th Fighter Squadron, USAAF, in the summer of 1943. The Thunderbolt was twice the weight of the Spitfire at normal loads (13,500lb compared to 6,750lb) and substantially larger. (USAAF)

Right, centre Sqn Ldr Jan Zumbach (centre) with two other members of No 303 Squadron beside his Spitfire when this famous Polish unit was based at Kirton-in-Lindsey, October 1942. The circular insignia beside the Donald Duck motif is that of Kosciusco, the city for which this squadron was named. (Via L. Gover)

Right, bottom Sqn Ldr Zumbach's Spitfire V EN951/'RF-D', seen here over Yorkshire in October 1942, served with four other squadrons and the Central Gunnery School before being pensioned off as an instructional airframe. (Via S. Clay)

Left, top The Spitfire IX, with its more powerful Merlin 60-series engine and two-stage supercharger, had a greatly enhanced performance. One of the first squadrons to be re-equipped with this model was No 611 ('West Lancashire') in July 1942. The CO between September 1942 and 5 February 1943—when he was shot down—was Sqn Ldr Hugo 'Sinker' Armstrong, an Australian, here photographed in the cockpit of a Spitfire at Biggin Hill on 8 December 1942. (RAF Museum)

Left, bottom Flt Lt William Crawford-Compton poses in the same Spitfire IX as his CO for Charles Brown on 8 December 1942 at Biggin Hill. At the time Bill Compton was the highest-scoring pilot in No 611 Squadron with ten confirmed victories, six of which had been made while flying with No 485 Squadron. A few weeks after this photograph was taken he was promoted to command No 64 Squadron, where he gained more successes. Following a lecture tour in the United States, he took No 145 Wing to the Continent, where yet further victories brought his total to 22. W. V. Crawford-Compton was the most highly decorated New Zealand fighter pilot of the war, with a DSO and Bar, DFC and Bar, Silver Star, Croix de Guerre and Legion d'Honneur. (RAF Museum)

Right, top A Spitfire IX of No 64 Squadron undergoing engine overhaul in a blister hangar on the north side of Fairlop, November 1942. No 64 was the first squadron in Fighter Command to receive the Mk IX. (IWM)

Right, bottom An unusually large gathering of ground staff on and around a Spitfire IX suggests that some were eager to get themselves in the picture—even 'Flight' had pedalled up on his bike to participate! The No 64 Squadron aircraft was pushed out of the hangar for this photo call so that full advantage could be taken of the bright winter sunshine. (IWM)

Far left, top The wreckage of a Ju 88 purported to have been shot down by the Canadian Spitfires of 'Johnny' Johnson's Wing lies not far from airstrip B-7 at Matragny, Normandy, 17 July 1944. The two French farmers are plaiting straw to bind clover bundles. (IWM)

Far left, centre Officers leading Wings carried their initials as identification letters on their allotted aircraft and some senior officers also followed this practice. This Spitfire IX, PV159, was visiting Debden and the letters 'RDE' identify the aircraft as that used by Wg Cdr R. Deacon Elliott, who was with 84 Group Support Unit at the time (spring 1945). (E. Richie)

Far left, bottom After VE-Day several RAF fighter squadrons made affiliation visits to fighter units of the USAAF. On 23 May 1945 twelve Spitfire IXs of No 313 Squadron, one of three three Czech-manned RAF fighter squadrons, flew to Debden. The rear inspection hatch was a useful place to stow kit—uniform in this case. (E. Richie)

Left, top A few cheery words from a fellow-pilot before the engine-start of Spitfire IX BR600/'SH-V' of No 64 Squadron at Fairlop. (IWM)

Left, bottom The RAF's top-scoring fighter pilot flying in north-west Europe was Wg Cdr James E. Johnson, with 38 victories. He is seen here on 31 July 1944 (at which time his total stood at 35) at Bazenville landing ground, Normandy, where he commanded No 127 Wing composed of three Canadian Spitfire squadrons. The dog is his pet labrador Sally. The decorations on 'Johnny' Johnson's tunic are a DSO with two Bars and a DFC with one Bar.

Left, top Spitfire LF.XVI SM348 of No 453 Squadron on a visit to Steeple Morden on 31 May 1945. This Canadian unit was then based at Hawkinge. By this date the white inner ring had been restored to the roundels displayed on the upper surface of the wings and the 'day fighter' identification band around the rear fuselage had been dispensed with. (A. Sloan)

Left, centre Fitters tightening coolant joints on the Griffon engine of a Spitfire XIVE at Melsbroek, Belgium, in December 1944. The 2,035hp-rated Griffon, giving this mark a maximum top speed of 439mph, led to the first squadrons equipped with this aircraft being used to chase and destroy V-1 flying bombs. (RAF Museum)

Left, bottom The huge five-blade propeller used on the Griffon engine of the Spitfire XIV. An RAF pilot is preparing to take off for a test flight. (RAF Museum)

Right, top The ultimate Spitfires: two F Mk 21s (LA232 and LA217) follow an F.22 (PK312) in this aerial photograph taken by Charles Brown for Vickers-Armstrong in March 1945 against a patchwork of fields at Gibbet Hill between Coventry and Kenilworth. One aircraft still has the old red and blue wing roundels, the application of which was officially discontinued in January that year. (RAF Museum)

Right, bottom Spitfire F.22 PK312 in March 1945. The only notable difference between the Spitfire F.21 and F.22 was the latter's cut-down rear fuselage and 'tear drop' canopy, affording the pilot enhanced rearward vision. Both the Mk 21 and the Mk 22 had a redesigned wing incorporating additional fuel cells to raise the total capacity from 85 gallons as in earlier models to 120 gallons; PK312 shows off this new stronger wing, and oil already stains the grey paintwork between the radiators of this first production aircraft. Both the F.21 and the F.22 were too late for combat employment. (RAF Museum)

Left, top and centre Of all RAF Fighter Command organizations, the most unusual was the Merchant Ship Fighter Unit. To combat attacks on Atlantic convoys by long-range *Luftwaffe* aircraft, a hurriedly designed but effective catapult was installed on the bows of a number of merchantmen to launch a Hurricane fighter. Pilots were volunteers and knew that after combat they faced a parchute descent into the sea unless land was in range. Fg Off Michael Lyne was one of the pilots who sailed in CAM ships (catapult armed merchant ships), and he took these unique colour photographs. The time is summer 1941 and the vessel is believed to be the *Empire Faith*. The Hurricane on the catapult, P3979, had previously seen action with Nos 87 and 213 Squadrons. The RAF support crew are seen at work in the second photograph, the four-man team consisting of fitter, rigger, radio mechanic and armourer. (AVM M. D. Lyne)

Left, bottom The CO of No 87 Squadron, Sqn Ldr Dennis Smallwood, in his personal Hurricane II BE500 *Cawnpore* I—named after a location in the United Provinces which donated the price of a squadron of Spitfires—is seen here flying from Charmy Down on 7 May 1942. The overall matt black finish for night fighters was soon to be removed as the Squadron was taken off night-fighting duties preparatory to its dispatch to North Africa in September to be employed in coastal defence. After overhaul, BE500 was shipped out to the Far East, where it was eventually SOC on 31 August 1944. (RAF Museum)

Right, top Built as a Hurricane IVD (tank-buster) with two 40mm cannon under each wing, KZ193 was temporarily converted to a Mk V by fitting it with a Merlin 32 engine driving a four-blade propeller for performance trials at Brooklands and Boscombe Down. It is seen here on 11 August 1943 flying near the Staines reservoirs. Visible behind the port wing is the original Heathrow aerodrome which would be transformed into London Airport in later years. This Hurricane was later returned to Mk IV status, assigned to No 164 Squadron at Warmwell and used for anti-shipping strikes. Still later it was sent to the Far East. It survived hostilities. (RAF Museum)

Right, bottom When it first appeared in 1939 the Westland Whirlwind held promise that was never realized, predominantly because of its underdeveloped Peregrine engines. Eventually only 116 were manufactured, equipping Nos 137 and 263 Squadrons before being withdrawn in 1943. P7048 went to No 137 Squadron in November 1941 and was damaged in May 1943. After repair it was used for experimental work at Boscombe Down and later by the manufacturer, being relegated to civil flying after the war but being dismantled in 1946. When photographed by Charles Brown over Mudford and the River Yeo, north-east of Yeovil, in August 1943, this Whirlwind was flying from the manufacturer's home airfield. (RAF Museum)

Far left, top The first US-built fighter to enter service with Fighter Command was the Bell Airacobra, with which No 601 Squadron re-equipped in August 1941; in October that year the Squadron displayed for the Press at its Duxford base. Here armourers uncomfortably draped with 20mm and .303 tracer rounds pose for the camera before CO Sqn Ldr E. J. Gracie's personal mount, *Skylark* XIII—which had the appropriate serial AH601. The removed nose panel reveals the positioning of the magazines for the cannon and machine guns. No 601's association with the Airacobra was short-lived, only a few sorties being flown before the type was withdrawn as unsuitable for offensive fighter operations. The red-winged sword device was based on the Squadron's badge. (Hulton)

Far left, bottom The Hawker Typhoon, originally hailed as a 'super-fighter' by the Press, was in reality a disappointment as an interceptor, in terms of both performance and reliablity. Engine and structural failure dogged the type in its early months of service. The first Typhoons went to No 56 Squadron at Duxford in September 1941 but it was the following May before the type was used operationally. This Typhoon IB, EK183, was one of many 'US-A'-coded aircraft used by No 56's COs. Seen here at Matlask on 21 April 1943, when Sqn Ldr T. H. V. Pheloung was in command, it was soon withdrawn for modification, later going to No 609 Squadron and ending its days as an instructional airframe at Cosford. (RAF Museum)

Left, top Fg Off C. T. 'Stimmie' Stimpson brings the 2,200hp Napier Sabre engine of Typhoon EK183 to life. At full power the Sabre enabled a Typhoon pilot to overhaul contemporary enemy fighters at low altitudes but it did not fare well in thinner air. The black and white striping under the wings was a type identification marking for anti-aircraft gunners, many of whom could see little difference in shape between the Typhoon and the FW 190. (RAF Museum)

Left, bottom At a dispersal point on the west side of Matlask, looking north towards the control tower, a fitter checks the ignition system of the Napier Sabre of a No 56 Squadron Typhoon, R8220/'US-D', on 21 April 1943; there were 48 spark plugs, two per cylinder, to check! Early Typhoon operations were dogged by problems with the Sabre, notably the seizure of the sleeve valves. By May 1943 engine changes were conducted after 30 hours. The use of new metals and manufacturing techniques eventually cured some of the problems but the Sabre remained a rather temperamental engine. (RAF Museum)

Left, top The Typhoon later proved to be a redoubtable fighter-bomber in ground-attack operations. *Dirty Dora* was the nickname of EK139/'HH-N' of No 175 Squadron seen here in a blast-walled dispersal point at Colerne in May 1943. The two dummy bombs were used for practice loadings on to wing racks. EK139 became a victim of engine failure with No 1 Squadron during a take-off from Lympne on 26 January 1944 when it crashed into a wood; fortunately the pilot survived. (IWM)

Left, bottom Another early Typhoon squadron, No 257, spent the best part of 1943 based at Warmwell with the principal tasks of intercepting the 'hit-and-run' *Luftwaffe* fighter-bomber raids against South Coast towns. Charles Brown, visiting the Squadron on 13 May 1943, took this and the other Kodachromes featuring No 257's aircraft that appear here. Typical of the unit's aircraft is Typhoon IB EJ927/'FM-Y', parked in the spring sunshine. This aircraft met its end exactly four months later with a belly landing at Gravesend following a tyre burst. (RAF Museum)

Right, top Flg Sgt Jack Mumford of No 257 Squadron. The small 'tear drop' blister on the top of the canopy held the rear-view mirror. (RAF Museum)

Right, centre Held by chocks and cranked up, EK172/'FM-M' emits a puff of smoke from the exhaust stacks; Sqn Ldr C. L. C. 'Bob' Roberts, commanding No 257 Squadron, is at the controls. The yellow chordwise band on the upper surface of each wing was an identification marking, occasioned by several Typhoons being mistaken for FW 190s. EK172 stayed with No 257 Squadron until April 1944—an amazingly long stretch with one operational unit. After modification, involving a new canopy and rocket projectile fittings, it was issued to No 181 Squadron, only to be destroyed on Eindhoven airfield by the *Luftwaffe* in the 1945 New Year's Day blitz. (RAF Museum)

Right, bottom A gathering of No 257 Squadron pilots on and around EK172/'FM-M'. Sitting on the wing, left to right, are P Off E. A. Tennant, Flt Sgt J. C. Mumford and Fg Off H. Y. Lao; standing, left to right, are Fg Off B. S. Spain, Fg Off S. J. Lovell, Sqn Ldr C. L. C. Roberts, Flt Sgt D. C. Campbell, Flt Lt G. F. Ball and P Off S. H. James. Lao was one of four Burmese pilots serving, appropriately, with this unit (named 'Burma Squadron', from funding by that country); sadly, he was killed in a bad-weather crash in the Netherlands on 20 January 1945. After the war Ted Tennant became a test pilot with Folland. (RAF Museum)

Left, top An armourer reloads the magazines of the port outer cannon. A full magazine had 140 rounds of 20mm ammunition, usually a mixture of high-explosive/incendiary and armour-piercing incendiary, fired at a rate of 600 rounds a minute. The aircraft is R8656/'FM-L' and the location a concrete standing in the north-west dispersal area at Warmwell. (RAF Museum)

Left, bottom For some reason the wartime censor masked out the serial number JP682 on this Typhoon seen high over the West Country on 24 August 1943. This fighter went on to serve with Nos 56, 197 and 183 Squadrons; it went missing in action on 24 February 1945 with Flt Lt Borham at the controls. (RAF Museum)

Right, top The Typhoon invariably aroused interest when it put down on a USAAF base. Harvey Mace, a P-51 Mustang pilot at Raydon, was sufficiently impressed to pose for a photograph before this No 486 Squadron aircraft, JP688/'SA-L', which 'dropped in' one bright January day in 1944. While serving with No 247 Squadron this Typhoon was lost on 24 October 1944 in operations over the Low Countries. (Harvey Mace)

Right, centre Engine trouble and hydraulic failure caused Flt Lt H. C. Taylor of No 440 Squadron to make a wheels-up landing at Nordholz on 8 July 1945. Raised, and with its undercarriage lowered, RB485/'I8-E' here stands forlorn among the summer flowers. The propeller spinner reposes nearby and displays the colourful markings used by this RCAF unit. (Stan Wyglendowski)

Right, bottom One of the limiting factors to the Typhoon's performance was its thick wing section. The manufacturers, Hawker, designed a completely new, thin-section, laminar-flow wing, semi-elliptical in shape, and with this wing and a re-designed tail the development was given a new name—Tempest. Various power units were mooted, but the first production model to reach the squadrons was the Tempest V with the Sabre, similar to that in the Typhoon, and performance and handling showed a great improvement over those of its predecessor. The first Tempests reached operational units in the spring of 1944 and the type eventually equipped eight active squadrons. Tempest V NV696, photographed here on 25 November 1944 while on a test flight from the Hawker factory at Langley, near Slough, went to No 222 Squadron the following month and survived hostilities. (RAF Museum)

Left, top All but one Tempest squadrons served with the 2nd Tactical Air Force on the Continent. The exception was No 501, which stayed in East Anglia to intercept V-1 flying bombs released from Heinkels over the North Sea. The Tempest V, with a maximum speed of 426mph, was the best suited of all RAF fighter types to overhaul these missiles. The photograph was taken on a dull day, 18 October 1944, at Bradwell Bay, the aircraft being EJ763/'SD-X'. (RAF Museum)

Left, centre Tempest V EJ650 of No 80 Squadron at Debden in the late summer of 1944. While operating from Coltishall on 25 September, this aircraft was hit by flak over Steenbergen, Holland, the pilot, Fg Off J. E. Wiltshire, bailing out and being taken prisoner. (E. Richie)

Left, bottom In the final year of hostilities the RAF re-equipped several of its fighter squadrons with Merlin-engine Mustangs, primarily for the long-range escort of bomber and coastal strike forces operating in daylight. One Wing, based at Andrews Field, was made up of Polish-manned squadrons with aircraft distinguished by a small representation of their country's national insignia, as on this Mustang III. (Stan Wyglendowski)

Right, top The Tempest II made use of the Bristol Centaurus radial engine rated at 2,520hp which, apart from raising top speed to 442mph, proved far more reliable than the fire- and seizure-prone Sabre. Although the first production aircraft was available in October 1944, a year was to pass before the first squadrons were re-equipped with Tempest IIs. The type was earmarked for South-East Asia, where air-cooled engines had been found to be hardier and less exacting in terms of maintenance than liquid-cooled powerplants. MW764 is seen here on a test flight from the manufacturer's airfield at Langley on 22 March 1945. (RAF Museum)

Right, centre The versatile Mosquito starred particularly well as a night fighter. The only RAAF night fighter squadron operating in Europe, No 456, made good use of the type, both in the defence of the United Kingdom and in intruder and Bomber Command support operations over the Continent. In this photograph of Mosquito IIF DD739/ 'RX-X', seen flying from Middle Wallop in June 1943, the wartime censor has scratched out the wing-tip antenna of the Airborne Interception (AI) radar. DD739 failed to return from a bomber support operation to Kassel on the night of 4 December 1943 with P Off J. L. May and his radar operator, Fg Off L. R. Parnell. (IWM)

Right, bottom The first jet-equipped squadron in the RAF, and the only one operational in the Second World War, was No 616. It received its first Gloster Meteor Is in July 1944 and moved to the Continent the following March, but there was never an opportunity to engage the enemy. Meteor III EE275/'YQ-Q', seen here parked on steel matting at B91, a few miles south of Nijmegen, during the third week of April 1945, was normally flown by Sqn Ldr D. A. Barr. (RAF Museum)

Above and right Rolls-Royce Derwent jet engines only produced a maximum 2,000lb of thrust, giving a top speed of around 480mph—not much in excess of that attainable by the latest propeller-driven fighters. The early British jet engines were, however, more reliable than those of the *Luftwaffe*'s aircraft. These two Charles Brown photographs show EE274/'YQ-P' of No 616 Squadron undergoing an engine-start, involving a compressor trolley to spin the turbine for firing-up. Both EE274 and EE275 endured to retirement through obsolescence in the postwar years. (RAF Museum)

Far right, top The RAF's second jet fighter, the De Havilland Vampire, powered by a DH Goblin, was starting to come off the production lines at English Electric's factory at Warton near the war's end, but the type did not enter service until the following spring. TG278, the third production aircraft, is seen here on a test flight on 23 August 1945. Retained by De Havilland, this Vampire was later modified with extended wings and re-engined with a DH Ghost; in the hands of test pilot John Cunningham it reached a record altitude of 59,446ft on 23 March 1948. (RAF Museum)

Coastal White and Grey

Early in the war aircraft for Coastal Command were being delivered in the Temperate Land Scheme, but soon the Temperate Sea Scheme, consisting of a disruptive pattern of colours described as Dark Slate Grey and Extra Dark Slate Grey, was introduced.

With the emphasis on the Battle of the Altantic, however, where Coastal Command joined with the Royal Navy to fight the U-boat menace, the function of the aircraft was anti-submarine warfare and their colouring required the best camouflage scheme for concealment from U-boat crews. After much experimentation with sea and sky colours, it was found that white was the most effective. From 1942 the main colour for general reconnaissance (as maritime reconnaissance was then called—an anachronism from pre-war days) was white, with only the strict plan view in the Temperate Sea Scheme upper-surface colours. During 1943 it was deemed that the disruptive camouflage patterning of the Sea Scheme was unnecessary and plan views could be a single-toned Dark Sea Grey.

While greys and whites were predominant, there were some variations in their application. For the Battle of the Atlantic, and for areas of the North Sea, Western Approaches and Biscay, aircraft had glossy white under surfaces and matt white sides, but for the Mediterranean and Persian Gulf areas grey sides were decreed with just the under surface glossy white.

Coastal strike aircraft normally were coloured in a Temperate Sea Scheme which, in their cases, covered all but the strict under surface of white, Sky, Azure Blue or black, according to their area and role.

Right Coastal Command was one of the success stories of the RAF, particularly in the so-called Battle of the Altantic, where it played a decisive part in the demise of the U-boat threat to Allied shipping. The stalwart of the Command throughout the war was the Short Sunderland flying boat, a military adaption of the pre-war Short passenger flying boats. Sunderland I L5802 was delivered to No 210 Squadron on 24 October 1938 and saw service with two other squadrons flying from Britain before being withdrawn for overhaul and assignment to No 95 Squadron, which was then based in West Africa. While being prepared at Pembroke Dock this aircraft was photographed bearing No 95 Squadron's code letters, possibly in the hope of misleading enemy intelligence into believing that the Squadron was still operating from the United Kingdom. Its age beginning to tell, L5802 was eventually retired to No 4 OTU at Alness on the Cromarty Firth, where it was wrecked in a night landing on 15/16 January 1943 when a float was torn off. (IWM)

Left, top Sunderland ML778/'NS-Z' of No 201 Squadron on its take-off run at Castle Archdale, Northern Ireland, 26 July 1945. The white finish was found to be the best air camouflage from surface viewing (such as from U-boats) and so it became the standard finish for all maritime reconnaissance units of Coastal Command from early 1943. (MOI)

Left, centre The crew of weather-worn Sunderland ML828/'RB-C' await the duty pinnace after a return from a sortie early in 1945. The location is Plymouth harbour, the RAF station being known as Mount Batten. The mid upper turrets were removed from most Sunderlands late the previous year. (Hulton)

Left, bottom Sunderland NJ265 on the step, engines at full power, about to break from the waters of Plymouth harbour, autumn 1944. This flying boat was assigned to No 10 Squadron, RAAF, a unit that had served with Coastal Command throughout the war in Europe from bases in Britain. (L. Gover)

Right, top The flight deck of a Sunderland (left); the Skipper has the controls while his Number Two scans a map. The pilots' reminder above the instrument panel reads: 'Are all hatches closed! Flaps must not be more than 1/3 out when taking off'. The US-built Catalina flying boat (right), while not as roomy as the Sunderland, had excellent endurance and gave valuable service to Coastal Command in its battle against the U-boats. Catalina 'F-Freddie', recently returned to Castle Archdale, is here being approached by a tender to collect the crew. (Douglas Fisher)

Right, bottom Other types that gave valiant service to Coastal Command in the anti-submarine long-range reconnaissance role were the Consolidated Liberator and Boeing Fortress. A limited number of Mk II, IIA and III Fortresses were obtained and used by three maritime reconnaissance and two meteorological squadrons, No 220 Squadron flying the type longer than any other, from July 1942 until January 1945. Fortress IIA FK186, flying with this squadron for most of this period, is seen here flying past a Hebridean island when based at Benbecula in May 1943. It was not fitted with ASV radar aerials at this date. (IWM)

Right, top Fg Off L. W. Taylor and crew, in typical pose before No 220 Squadron's FL462/'W', study maps in the all too rare sunshine at Benbecula, May 1943. Taylor wears the darker blue uniform of the RAAF. This Fortress IIA hit trees while trying to land in bad weather at Gosport on 22 January 1945. (IWM)

Right, bottom For short-range reconnaissance, a militarized version of the Lockheed 14 airliner, named Hudson, served with several squadrons of Coastal Command during the early years of hostilities. This trio, photographed by Charles Brown on 15 December 1941, were on the strength of No 6 OTU at Thornaby. All these aircraft eventually came to grief. The centre Hudson, V9032/'OD-N', stalled on take-off at Thornaby three days after this photograph was taken, on 18 December 1941. The others were passed to No 1404 Meteorological Flight late in 1942, where the lower aircraft in the picture, V9029/'OD-J' was damaged and SOC on 1 February 1943. The third Hudson, V8986/'OD-K', went missing 30 miles south-east of the Scilly Isles on 10 February 1943, after flying a total of 652 hours. (RAF Museum)

Far right, top Designed as a bomber but not required for that purpose, the Vickers Warwick was adapted for other roles. The Warwick V only equipped one squadron of Coastal Command, No 179, operating out of St Eval on anti-submarine patrols. This mark was sent mainly overseas to equip squadrons of the RAF and SAAF. Several months' exposure to the elements had given PN811/'OZ-V' a decidedly worn look when this photograph was taken on 15 December 1945 against the background of a raging ocean. (RAF Museum)

Far right, bottom The Bristol Beaufort torpedo strike aircraft achieved many successes against enemy shipping, albeit at some cost. In December 1941 a detachment of six Beauforts each from Nos 217 and 86 Squadrons was sent to St Eval to stand by for a possible break-out by the battlecruiser *Scharnhorst* from its French harbour. While at St Eval, on 14 January 1942, No 217's Beauforts were the subject of a Press photographic visit. Here a pilot, thought to be Flt Lt A. J. H. Finch DFC, is about to settle in the cockpit of Beaufort I N1012/'MW-S' prior to flying for photographers. (IWM)

Right Beauforts N1173/'MW-E' and
AW242/'MW-B' make a low pass along the
Cornish coastline, 14 January 1942. (IWM)
Below Another view of No 217 Squadron's
'MW-E' and 'MW-B'. N1173 was lost in the
North Sea on 12 February 1942 during the
'Channel Dash' by *Scharnhorst*, *Gneisenau* and
Prinz Eugen. AW242 flew into a hill at
Auchowrie, six miles north-west of Edzell, on
8 March 1942 (IWM)
Far right, **bottom** Beaufort I L9878/'MW-R'
over Cornwall in January 1942. A long-serving
aircraft, it was eventually SOC in May 1943.
(RAF Museum)

Left, top The Handley Page Hampden equipped the bomber squadrons of No 5 Group for the first two years of hostilities. As they were replaced by types more suited to the Command's purpose, many Hampdens went to Coastal Command where the aircraft's long bomb bay was able to accommodate a torpedo. AT137/'UB-T' of No 455 Squadron RAAF is depicted here in May 1942 when based at Leuchars. The aircraft was damaged on 8 June that year and declared to be beyond economical repair. (RAF Museum)

Left, centre Air Sea Rescue (ASR), both aircraft and marine units, came under Coastal Command and was one of the roles for the Warwick, which had been designed as a bomber. This example in Coastal Command's white dress, BB285, photographed on 13 July 1943 while with the ASR Training Unit, was to come to an untimely end when it hit a tree after take-off from Hurn on 20 November the same year. (RAF Museum)

Left, bottom Mosquitos equipped several Coastal Command strike squadrons near the end of the war. The Wing at Banff harried enemy shipping off the Norwegian and Danish coasts. Its commander was Gp Capt J. W. Max Aitken, son of Lord Beaverbrook, the first Minister of Aircraft Production. In the background are the ricks of Hopetown Farm. (RAF Museum)

Right, top Three-inch rockets with 60lb HE/SAP heads being loaded on to PZ438/'NE-F', a Mosquito FB.VI of No 143 Squadron, at Banff in February 1945. Four of these missiles were carried under each wing. At the time No 143 Squadron Mosquitos were identified by yellow-outlined code letters and yellow spinners. (RAF Museum)

Right, bottom Many a well-worn Spitfire ended its days as an ASR spotter. Spitfire V AB981/'MY-T', served with five squadrons of Fighter Command from 1941 to 1943—Nos 403, 165, 501, 504 and 129. It was then modified for ASR work and sent to No 278 Squadron's detachment at Martlesham Heath, where it was captured on Kodachrome one bright February day in 1945. (Herb Rutland)

Right, top Air Sea Rescue Type 2 high-speed launch No 137 at full speed, summer 1943. Known as a 'Whaleback', it was 63ft long and capable of 36kts. It was built by the British Power Boat Company at Hythe, Hampshire, entered service in November 1941 and was based in northern Scotland and the Orkneys before coming south and being transferred to the Mediterranean area. (USAAF)

Far right WAAF assistants check the inventory of equipment on newly commissioned launch No 2562 before its handing over to an operational unit in February 1942. A 68ft Hants & Dorset Mk I built by British Power Boats, this craft served with ASR units at Calshot and Felixstowe in the United Kingdom. (IWM)

Right, bottom ASR launch No 2626 on service trials with 238 MU in the Solent. Built by British Power Boats of Hythe, she was taken into service in July 1943 and subsequently sent to the Far East. (RAF Museum)

Reconnaissance Hues

Fighter aircraft adapted for photographic reconnaissance were usually finished in the Temperate Land Scheme, but it soon became evident that sub-stratosphere flying needed a special camouflage scheme of its own. As these high-fliers were unlikely to be spotted from above when operational, an overall colour scheme was acceptable, but the difficulty was in deciding on a particular hue. Making an outward journey under cover of darkness to be over the area to be photographed in the brightness of dawn led to some aircraft to be finished in overall pink. Various hues were tried before standardization on a deep blue, to merge with what poets have described as 'the deep blue vault of the heavens'. This shade became officially known as PR Blue and with this finish only the red and blue roundel was displayed as it was thought that white might reflect in the strong sunlight of the upper regions.

While PR Blue was logical for aircraft operating above cloud, where it existed, on their flight to cloud-free areas for photography, the camouflage was often comprised by contrails streaming behind the aircraft, pointing out to ground observers the course they were taking with, in some cases, the machine itself invisible.

For the low-level army co-operation aircraft, the Temperate Scheme was applied to aircraft like the Lysander and the early Mustangs. An exception were the Air Observation Post aircraft in that the upper surface camouflage scheme appropriate to the theatre of operations was applied overall. In the final stages of the war, the main PR aircraft (such as Spitfires) were in some cases allowed a highly polished natural metal finish so that the aircraft might achieve the highest possible speeds.

Right, top A purpose-designed aircraft for army support was the Westland Lysander, which entered service in 1938 and was soon affectionately known as 'the Lizzie'. Lysander I L4798 was serving with No 16 Squadron as 'KJ-S' when this photograph was taken at Cranwell a few weeks before the outbreak of hostilities. The aircraft later served with No 239 Squadron before being shipped out to India, where it ended its days. (AVM M. D. Lyne)

Right, bottom The Battle of France in May and June 1940 showed the Lysander to be far too slow and vulnerable for ground support and a new concept was born whereby tactical reconnaissance would be undertaken by fast fighter-type aircraft with fixed camera installations to back up the pilot's observations. Early in 1942 the North American Mustang was allotted this task and eventually sixteen squadrons re-formed, or were re-equipped, with this excellent aircraft. No 2 Squadron at Sawbridgeworth was one of the first, and its Mustangs were shown to the Press on 24 July 1942. This views shows the location of the backward-facing F24 camera just aft of the cockpit, with young P Off Peter Tonkin preparing to start the engine. (RAF Museum)

Left, top The same aircraft, AG550/'XV-U', strains against the chocks as the engine is run up. The armament of two .50-calibre Brownings, protruding from the lower engine cowling and synchronized to fire through the propeller arc, can be clearly seen. The Mustang also carried one .50-calibre Browning (here sealed with white tape) and two .30-calibre machine guns (sealed with red tape) in each wing. (RAF Museum)

Left, centre AG550/'XV-U' taxies out at Sawbridgeworth. The 1,150hp-rated Allison engine allowed a top speed of nearly 390mph at low altitude but, lacking supercharging, was unsuitable for high-altitude combat operations. For this reason the Mustang I was not issued to day fighter squadrons, despite having twice the range of the Spitfire. AG550 hit a hill at Kimmeridge, Dorset, while returning from a sortie in foggy conditions on 26 May 1943. The pilot was killed. (RAF Museum)

Left, bottom Mustang I AG633/'XV-E' of No 2 Squadron flying south-west just to the east of Great Dunmow, Essex. The dwelling visible under the port wing is Merks Hall. Another bad-weather victim, this aircraft overshot and crashed while trying to land at Sawbridgeworth on 29 October 1942. (RAF Museum)

Right, top In the immediate post-war period there was an increased requirement for air photography by the Allied occupation forces in Germany as part of the policing activities and three RCAF fighter squadrons were formed into No 39 Reconnaissance Wing, which operated a number of Spitfire FR.XIVs at B156 Lüneberg during the summer of 1945. The camera port can be seen ahead of the roundel on this aircraft, which is undergoing refuelling. (CAF)

Right, bottom The vital requirement for regular photographic coverage of enemy-held territory quickly led to a buoyant photographic reconnaissance organization, administratively under Coastal Command but with an interpretation centre at Medmenham, near Henley-on-Thames, which aided or served all Commands. Most of the photographic sorties in hostile airspace were flown by fast unarmed adaptations of fighter aircraft, notably the Spitfire. Spitfire PR.XI EN654, here seen on 17 October 1943, went to No 16 Squadron which was then based at Hartford Bridge. The overall finish was the shade known as 'PR Blue'. (RAF Museum)

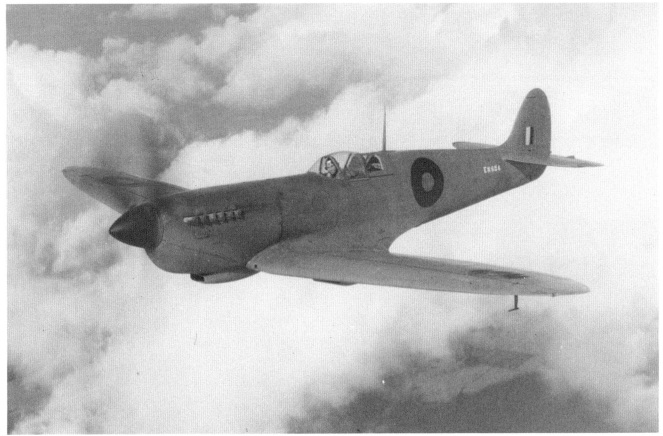

Left, top The other main type used for high-altitude photographic reconnaissance was the Mosquito, the PR.XVI becoming the standard model for this duty. NS777 served only with No 140 Squadron, which operated from B58 Melsbroek, Belgium, during the last seven months of the war in Europe. This photograph was taken in December 1944 when the aircraft was parked outside an improvised hangar disguised as a farm barn. (RAF Museum)

Left, bottom When the Allies invaded North-West Africa in the late autumn of 1942, No 544 Squadron at Benson had its 'B' Flight at Gibraltar carrying out high-altitude reconnaissance in the region. On 23 December that year the two Spitfire PR.IVs of the Flight, BR668 and BS491, were sent to Marrakesh for secret operations and the aircraft were photographed en route when they put down at Casablanca to refuel. Flt Sgt J. E. Thomson was the pilot of BS491. This Spitfire operated from Gibraltar for a year. In the autumn of 1943 the Flight was transferred to No 541 Squadron and on 16 December BS491 was flown to Britain. An undercast prevailed when the pilot, Flt Lt R. P. Johnson, reached south-east England and, as fuel was almost depleted, he apparently elected to bale out. In so doing he is thought to have struck the tail for his body was found with an unopened parachute a mile from where the Spitfire crashed at Wraxall, Somerset.

Right, top to bottom Mosquito PR.XVIs of No 680 Squadron at San Savero, around September 1944 (top). The red and white tail striping was a type identity marking aimed at preventing the Mosquito from being mistaken for the Me 410 by trigger-happy Allied fighter pilots. The black and white fuselage banding was applied as a 'friendly' recognition marking during the Allied invasion of southern France. No 60 Squadron SAAF also operated PR.XVIs from San Savero and NS644/'G' and NS691/'H' (second photograph) both survived hostilities. The unit's aircraft were distinguishable from those of No 680 Squadron RAF by having yellow-painted propeller spinners. In the third photograph, Spitfire PR.XIs of 'A' Flight, No 682 Squadron, are seen parked and with engines cloaked at arid San Savero, around September 1944. PA910/'B', in the foreground, joined the Squadron in July 1944 and remained with it for over a year. Four Spitfires of No 682 Squadron are seen at San Savero in the bottom photograph. 'E' is a PR.XI and 'F' a PR.XIX with a Griffon engine, which gave greater speed, ceiling and range over the Merlin-powered PR.XI. Camera ports adjacent to the fuselage roundel can be clearly seen in this photograph. (Via Bruce Robertson)

Transport Tones

Transport aircraft used by various Commands at home and overseas were finished in colours appropriate to their location. Later in the war, when long-range transports were crossing zones where different schemes appertained, they took on the colours appropriate to their unit base.

Civil aircraft were camouflaged to the same schemes as service aircraft, mainly for concealment at their bases. But as they visited, or staged through, neutral countries such as Portugal, Sweden and Turkey, their large registration letters were picked out in silver paint and underlined with red, white and blue bars.

Training gliders and tugs had conspicuous yellow undersurfaces with diagonal black bands, as the photographs show. The object was to warn other aircraft and deter fighter pilots from practising approach attacks to aircraft trailing or attached to a towline.

Right, top Transportation of service personnel or cargo by air was not a priority in the pre-war expansion of the RAF. With the outbreak of hostilities most civilian airline and transport aircraft were impressed and obsolete bombers were converted for the task. A more pressing need was to provide transport for airborne forces. When they could be spared from Bomber Command, Whitleys each able to carry up to ten paratroops formed the initial equipment of squadrons designated for this purpose. The paratroops seen are dropping over Netheravon from a Whitley of No 295 Squadron during a practice recorded as taking place on 2 October 1942. (IWM) **Right, bottom** Airborne troops check and adjust equipment before entering Whitley 'PX-G' of No 295 Squadron at Netheravon on 2 October 1942.

Left, top Paratroops on parade in front of Building 6, a VR hangar at Ringway, the home of No 1 Parachute Training School. A Lancaster and a Handley Page Harrow can be seen in the background. This photograph was probably taken during a presentation on 20 October 1942. (IWM)

Left, bottom The first glider for carrying airborne troops, the General Aircraft Hotspur, was used solely for training. These Hotspurs are of the Glider Pilot Exercise Unit at Netheravon with six-man parties of 1st Airborne Division Paratroops boarding, probably on 13 October 1942. In the background are the towing Hawker Hectors of No 296 Squadron. Both Hotspur HH541/'Y1' and BT744/'B1' endured the often hard handling involved with trainees to outlast the war. (IWM)

Right, top Paratroops entering Hotspur HH541 at Netheravon—a tight squeeze in this durable glider of largely wood and canvas construction. (IWM)

Right, centre The Airspeed Horsa became the standard assault glider. This training example, DP288, has yellow and black underwing stripes, indicating its towed status in No 21 Heavy Glider Conversion Unit at Brize Norton. The paratroops are taking part in a Press Facility Day exercise on 24 June 1943. (IWM)

Right, bottom Horsa I LG850, of No 22 Heavy Glider Conversion Unit, demonstrates the mid-fuselage separation of this type, which enabled large pieces of equipment to be unloaded speedily. The occasion was a Royal visit to Netheravon on 19 May 1944. Part of an A-type hangar is visible in the background. (IWM)

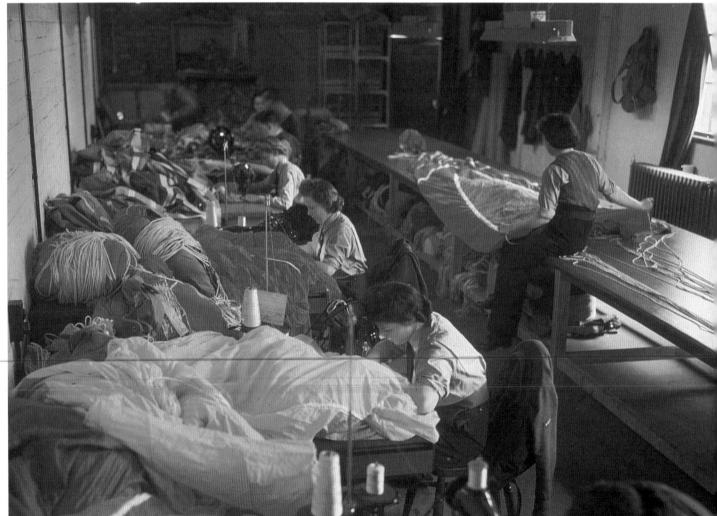

Left, top An unexpected visitor at Steeple Morden in March 1945 was Horsa PF697, which had become separated from its tug. The Horsa was a heavy glider requiring a much longer landing run than the Waco CG-4A used by US forces and by the RAF as the Hadrian. (A. Sloan)

Left, bottom WAAFs repair and pack parachutes for the airborne forces, May 1944. The different-coloured canopies were used to identify the general content of the panniers to which the parachutes would be attached. (IWM)

Right, top The General Aircraft Hamilcar was the giant of assault gliders and could carry a small tank or armoured car. This line-up at Tarrant Rushton on 12 October 1944 is ready for a training operation with the Halifax tugs of Nos 298 and 644 Squadrons. (RAF Museum)

Right, centre A view from beside the cockpit of a Hamilcar looking down the line-up. The bracing on the tail surfaces prevented oscillation and possible damage in turbulence. (RAF Museum)

Right, bottom A No 298 Squadron Halifax V prepares to take off from a Tarrant Rushton runway in the hazy sunshine of 12 October 1944. Because of the poor visibility, mobile two-strip sodium lamps have been positioned as visual aids to pilots on approach. (RAF Museum)

Left, top The Stirling was adapted for glider towing, the nose and top turrets being dispensed with. This Stirling V, LK554 of No 299 Squadron, is on a visit to Bury St Edmunds, summer 1945. (Air Force Academy)

Left, centre Another view of 'X9-M' from the rear, clearly showing the high angle of incidence of a Stirling's wing when tail-down on the ground. (Air Force Academy)

Left, bottom RAF Transport Command was not formed until March 1943 and eventually embraced most transport units, including Ferry Command (which, as the name suggests, had been formed to administer the collection and delivery of aircraft, predominantly transatlantic from the United States). Many of the early Consolidated Liberators received by the RAF were employed as ferry transports. One veteran was AL627, seen here over Montreal nearing the end of a flight from Prestwick in May 1944. (IWM)

Right, top The Liberator was built in greater numbers than any other US or British bomber, a total of 19,256 being produced. This is the fifth production aircraft, AM262, which, like the other five in the first batch, lacked the self-sealing fuel tanks deemed essential for combat. AM262 became a transport, first with No 1425 Flight on the transatlantic ferry routes and then with the British Overseas Airways Corporation. Here it is seen over North America prior to delivery in 1941. (USAAF)

Right, centre No 168 Squadron RCAF was specially formed to carry mail to and from Canadian service personnel in Europe and the Mediterranean war theatres, and for this task it was initially equipped with six well-worn Boeing Fortresses. No 9202 (a B-17F) began transatlantic mail flights to Prestwick on 22 December 1943, making some 70 crossings during the following 22 months. It was destroyed and all five crew members were killed in a crash near Münster, Germany, on 4 November 1945, while flying a load of penicillin from Canada to Warsaw. In this photograph the aircraft is seen at its Rockcliffe, Ontario, base. (RCAF)

Right, bottom Although ostensibly a civil organization, BOAC was staffed largely by personnel detached from the RAF. A few of the pre-war Imperial Airways aircraft were employed for a period, including this Armstrong Whitworth Ensign, G-ADSU *Euterpe*, seen under maintenance at Whitchurch on 15 October 1942. Used on the Cairo–Calcutta section of the Australia route for most of the war, it fell into disrepair and was eventually cannibalized for parts at Almaza in February 1945. (IWM)

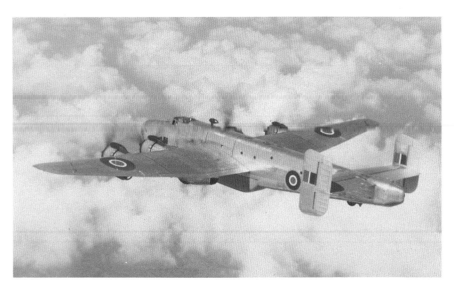

Left, top Whitchurch was Base 'A' for BOAC in 1942 and at one time some sixty impressed airliners were to be seen there. Included was this former KLM DC-3, its name *Zilverreiger* (Silver Heron) no longer appropriate to the camouflage paintwork it had received. When this photograph was taken at Whitchurch on 15 October 1942 the aircraft was serving BOAC as G-AGBE. *Zilverreiger* was returned to KLM after the war. The aircraft in the background are Whitleys modified for passenger use by BOAC. (RAF Museum)

Left, centre The Douglas DC-4 was one of the most advanced airliners of its day and during the war was produced as a USAAF transport under the designation C-54 Skymaster. Ten were obtained by the RAF, deliveries commencing in February 1945. Skymaster I KL980 (ex-42-72532), seen here disgorging passengers at Brussels, was used on the Atlantic routes. Being Lend-Lease, it was returned to the US in July 1946. (IWM)

Left, bottom Handley Page produced a special transport version of the Halifax, the C.VIII, with a pannier type extension below the bomb bay for cargo. However, with large numbers of surplus USAAF cargo aircraft available in the immediate post-war years, the Halifax was not an attractive proposition. PP285, photographed here against a backdrop of spring clouds on 16 May 1945, was later returned to Handley Page at the company's Radlett airfield for experimental work and then stored at No 58 MU until scrapped in March 1948. (RAF Museum)

Right, top The Stirling V was used for general transport as well as being employed by the airborne forces. PK148 was an aircraft of No 51 Squadron at Stradishall in the summer of 1945 and one of the first to be delivered in natural metal finish. Seen at an airfield in Germany, PK148 was later sold to a Belgian company and finally scrapped at Thame in 1948. The identification letters are based on the wireless transmission codes. (Byron Trent)

Right, bottom The RAF's first true British-designed transport was the Avro York, a development of the Lancaster bomber. York C.1 MW185 was allotted to No 246 Squadron when photographed in Germany in the summer of 1945. After service with other RAF units, this freighter was sold for civilian use in September 1952 and later went to Canada, where it was damaged beyond repair in 1958. (Byron Trent)

Left, top A VIP Douglas Dakota served to transport HM King George VI on his visit to the British forces in the Netherlands on 12 October 1944. To meet him were Field Marshal Sir Bernard Montgomery and Air Vice Marshals Coningham and Broadhurst of the 2nd Tactical Air Force. (IWM)

Left, bottom In addition to its training role, the Avro Anson was used extensively as a light transport and communications aircraft in the later war years. This Anson I is being flown by pilots of the Air Transport Auxiliary. The inertia starter on the port engine has just been released as the aircraft prepares to leave North Weald, 4 May 1942. (RAF Museum)

Right, top to bottom An impressed Lockheed 12 (top) used for VIP transport (and carrying the Duke of Gloucester when this photograph was taken at Polebrook in May 1943). The next photograph shows a Miles Mentor, L4428, at Cranwell in the summer of 1939. The Mentor was the military version of the popular Nighthawk sportsplane, of which 45 were acquired for communications purposes. L4428 served first with No 1 Electrical and Wireless School. It ended its days at RAF Usworth, being SOC 19 January 1942. A popular communications aircraft, the Percival Proctor (third photograph) was derived from the makers' Vega Gull sports aircraft of 1935. In total, 1,143 were built during the war, the Proctor IV being completely redesigned and structurally strengthened. This is the Mk IV prototype, LA586, over Luton on 12 April 1944. The De Havilland Dominie was another pre-war civilian design adopted for military use as a light communications aircraft and radio trainer, over 500 being built for these purposes. This example (bottom photograph) was a visitor to Mount Farm in 1944. The brightly painted Jeep served to lead visitors to a parking place. (S. Clay/AVM M. D. Lyne/RAF Museum/R. Astrella)

Shades of Sand and Sea

In the Middle East and North Africa a disruptive camouflage pattern for the upper and side surfaces of aircraft still appertained, but in the brown shades of Dark Earth and Middle Stone, the latter usually being called mid-stone. Undersurfaces, reflecting the brighter skies of the Mediterranean areas, were Azure Blue.

SAAF units serving under RAF overall command, having aircraft supplied from RAF maintenance units, had the same finishes, even to the standard RAF roundels. However, in some cases SAAF personnel did substitute the orange of the Union's colours for the British red, while SAAF transport and communications aircraft coming from the Union would permanently display the Union colours of orange, white and blue in the standard British roundel form.

When the main sphere of operations shifted from North Africa to Italy, the Temperate Land Scheme camouflage became more appropriate than the Middle East Scheme, which was thus no longer applied.

Right, top Egypt was the hub of RAF Middle East activity and the favourite landmarks to reconnoitre on a 'local flight' were the Pyramids. Here Lockheed Hudson AE626 of the Middle East Communications Flight circles these historic monuments in the summer of 1942. (IWM)
Right, bottom Pushing up a cloud of dust, Beaufighter IF V8318, 'F-Freddie' of No 252 Squadron, moves out at Magrun, April 1943. (IWM)

Left, top Morning ablutions in the Libyan Desert: a No 252 Squadron Beaufighter crew at improvised washbasins, with water from a jerry can. In the all-male establishment little heed was given to lack of clothing at such times, although the officer cleaning his teeth has acknowledged the need for modesty before a camera and made use of a towel. The tent has a double canopy, the purpose of the outer canvas being to absorb the sun's heat. (IWM)

Left, bottom Work on a Beaufighter's Hercules engines at Magrun, April 1943. Each of the 14-cylinder, two-row, air-cooled, sleeve-valve, radial engines produced in excess of 1,500hp at maximum power, giving the Beaufighter a top speed of between 300 and 325mph depending on altitude. (IWM)

Right, top A Beaufighter IF of No 252 Squadron making a low pass over Magrun landing ground. Though a rugged and versatile aircraft, the Beaufighter was found to suffer from longitudinal instability at low speeds, a problem overcome in later models by giving 12° of dihedral to the tailplane. (IWM)

Right, bottom This No 252 Squadron Beaufighter, straining at the chocks, has an F14 camera in its nose. (IWM)

Right The most eye-catching among the various fighter types operating in North Africa were the 'shark-nosed' Curtiss Kittyhawks of No 112 Squadron. Here the pilots of FR472/'GA-L' and FR440/'GA-V' are watching for the leader of the trio to move out. The unit's base at the time, April 1943, was Medenine. (IWM)

Below A highly decorative Kittyhawk II of No 112 Squadron taxies through scrub. The ground crewman on the wing directs the pilot, whose view ahead is hindered by the aircraft's nose when tail-down. (IWM)

Far right, bottom The CO of No 112 Squadron and his two Flight Commanders discuss a course. Sqn Ldr G. W. Garton holds the map; the pilot on his right is believed to be Capt E. C. Saville SAAF, the 'A' Flight CO, and the officer on his left is thought to be Flt Lt L. Usher, the 'B' Flight CO. (IWM)

Left, top Spitfire Vs of the Canadian No 417 Squadron in loose formation over the Tunisian Desert in April 1943. The red propeller spinner was a theatre marking for day-flying Allied aircraft, although it was not used by every unit. (IWM)

Left, bottom Flt Lt W. H. Pentland awaiting start-up at Goubrine, Tunisia, April 1943. BR195 survived hostilities and was passed to the Greeks in September 1945. (IWM)

Right, top Even in the desert no self-respecting barber would go about his work without a gown for his client. Here the recipient of 'short back and sides' is the Medical Officer of No 417 Squadron, Flt Lt H. J. F. Joncas. The five-gallon can served many purposes in the desert, a seat being but one. (IWM)

Right, bottom The ground crews of No 417 Squadron in and around an overloaded Jeep at Goubrine, April 1943. One suspects that the cameraman suggested they act as if pushing, but, if so, the result is none too convincing! (IWM)

Left, top Spitfire boneyard at Gabes, Tunisia: JG726/'AN-L' of No 417 Squadron is being cannibalized for parts. The aircraft was scrapped after colliding with a Hudson during take-off on 19 April 1943. (IWM)

Left, bottom Another wreck, that of EN459, bears the markings of No 145 Squadron. This was an aircraft of the Polish Flight operating as part of the Squadron from March to June 1943 with Spitfire IXs for high-altitude duties. The Flight's aircraft carried numeric plane-in-squadron identities, and 'ZX-1' was the usual mount of Sqn Ldr S. F. Skalski. On 6 April 1943 Flt Lt E. Horbaczewski shot down a Bf 109 with this Spitfire but was then attacked by another 109, as a result of which his engine caught fire. The fire subsided and he was able to glide for a crash-landing at Gabes. (IWM)

Right, top A No 601 Squadron Spitfire V, believed to be ER207/'UF-K', lands against a background of the Tunisian town of Gabes in early April 1943. (IWM)

Right, bottom The South African Air Force had a strong participation in the air war waged at the north end of the Continent, and a not infrequent visitor to that area was the Supreme Commander of the Union Defence Forces, Field Marshal Jan Smuts. His flying visits were often made in an ex-South African Airways Lockheed Lodestar, which retained its natural metal finish when it became No 234 of the SAAF. (IWM)

Left, top No 40 Squadron SAAF, equipped with 'clipped-wing' Spitfire Vs, served in a ground support role. Here ER622/'WR-D' accompanied by 'WR-C' patrols over the Tunisian battle front ready to be called in for an 'air shoot' by the Army. (IWM)

Left, centre The SAAF pilot of ER622 confers with his 'No 2' back in the parched grass at Gabes, April 1943. (IWM)

Left, bottom Hurricane IIDs of No 6 Squadron rolling out at Gabes soon after noon on 6 April 1943 for a 'tank-busting' raid. The aircraft carry a 40mm cannon under each wing for ground attack. No 6 was the last combat unit with Hurricanes in North Africa. For HW313/'S', however, this was to be the first and last combat sortie: it was brought down by intense ground fire near Sfax, although the pilot, Fg Off T. I. Petersen, escaped to rejoin his squadron (IWM)

Right, top A Hurricane tank-buster of No 6 Squadron demonstrates the effect of its firepower on an abandoned enemy tank in Tunisia. (IWM)

Right, centre The wreckage of a Ju 52/3m transport destroyed on Gabes airfield; beyond, a convoy of RAF transports moves in. The photograph was taken the day after this airfield was captured at the end of March 1943. (IWM)

Right, bottom The SAAF had several bomber squadrons operating in North Africa, two equipped with Douglas Bostons. Here the engines are being run up on Boston 'S-Sugar' of No 24 Squadron SAAF, a unit commanded by Lt Col R. A. Blackwell, DFC. (IWM)

Left, top Bostons of No 24 Squadron SAAF lined up at Zuara, Tripolitania, in March 1943. The nearest aircraft, AL683/'V', was SOC a year later. (IWM)

Left, bottom A formation of No 24 Squadron SAAF Bostons over the Tunisian coastline. The Dark Earth and Middle Stone camouflage of these aircraft blends well with the arid desert colours below. (IWM)

Right, top The same SAAF Bostons against the blue of the Mediterranean. (IWM)

Right, bottom While a formation flies overhead, other Martin Baltimores of No 223 Squadron stir up the dust on a Tunisian airfield (probably Ben Gardane), late March 1943. The Baltimore gave valiant service in the medium bomber role, equipping two RAF and three SAAF squadrons at maximum inventory during the summer of 1943. (IWM)

Left A Flight Lieutenant bomb-aimer of No 223 Squadron over his bomb sight in Baltimore 'N-Nan', April 1943. The open bomb-bay doors give a glimpse of general-purpose 250-pounders. The Baltimore's usual load totalled 2,000lb. (IWM)

Right, top A cluster of 250lb bombs dumped among the desert stones. It all looks rather casual, but there was none of the sophisticated handling equipment that was available in Europe and the missiles had to be moved by hand. The armourer is checking tail fixings prior to loading. (IWM)

Right, bottom Malta, for long beleaguered, became a plank in the air offensive to capture Sicily in the summer of 1943. On the day the invasion was launched, 10 July, the AOC-in-C Middle East, Air Chief Marshal Sir W. Sholto Douglas, was photographed consulting with the AOC Malta, Air Vice-Marshal Sir Keith Park, in the garden at HQ. Park, apparently favouring Brylcreem, is enjoying a holder-fixed cigarette. (IWM)

Left, top Chocks away! Air Vice-Marshal Keith Park about to taxi out in his personal Spitfire V to mark the opening of Malta's new airstrip to Safi before a throng of civilian onlookers. Marks of rank are the non-regulation white flying helmet and the AVM pennant on the fuselage. The opening ceremony had been performed by Field Marshal Lord Gort VC, Malta's Governor. (IWM)

Left, bottom Air Vice-Marshal Park climbs away after his ceremonial take-off, 15 May 1943, watched by RAF personnel, Basuto and Mauritian troops and Maltese civilian workers. (IWM)

Right, top Non-regulation transport: a red MG sports car with Air Vice-Marshal Keith Park (at the wheel) and Air Vice-Marshal Arthur Coningham, AOC Desert Air Force, during the latter's visit to Malta in June 1943. (IWM)

Right, centre With a Valetta in the background, Beaufighter IVF 'F-Freddie' of No 272 Squadron is here on the move at Luqa. A Coastal Command unit, No 272 equipped its Beaufighters with racks for underwing stores. (IWM)

Right, bottom A flight of No 272 Squadron Beaufighters patrols off Malta, early June 1943. These Coastal aircraft were modified to carry a .303 machine gun in the rear observer's position. (IWM)

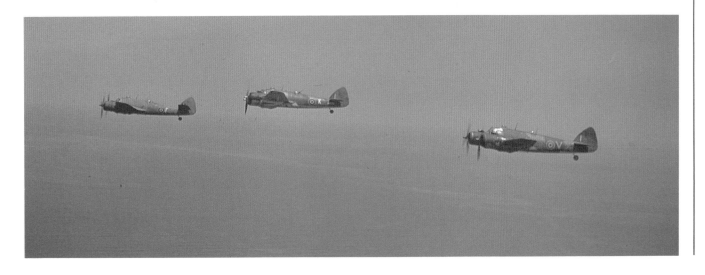

Left, top and centre Beaufighter 'Y-York', T5173 of No 272 Squadron, affording escort for a convoy bound for Tripoli on 30 May 1943. The Squadron was then based at Ta Kali. (IWM)

Left, bottom Resting here in blast-wall-protected Dispersal Point 125 at Luqa in June 1943 is a Bristol Beaufort II of No 39 Squadron. At the time of the photograph this unit was about to convert to Beaufighters. (IWM)

Right The night defence of Malta was chiefly the duty of No 23 Squadron, which had been sent out from the United Kingdom in December 1942 with its Mosquito IIs. Here, with an audience more for the camera than for him, the CO and his navigator arrive at Mosquito 'P-Peter'. The four 20mm cannon are 'corked' to prevent the ingress of dirt. (IWM)

Above No 23 Squadron Mosquito II DZ231/'YP-R', here flying over the island in June 1943, still retains its Temperate camouflage of green and grey disruptive patterning on the upper surfaces. (IWM)

Right Mosquito 'YP-R' about to attack a target on a rock outcrop in the Mediterranean during a gunnery practice flight, June 1943. At the time No 23 Squadron was going over to offensive operations against ground targets in Italy and Sicily. (IWM)

Far right, top and bottom After Sicily the Allies secured southern Italy but were brought to a virtual standstill by German defences in the mountainous central area before Rome. Among the air units established in southern Italy during the winter of 1943–44 was No 241 Squadron, armed with Spitfire IXs for tactical reconnaissance duties but also engaging in fighter escort and ground attack sorties. Here two of its aircraft, MA425/'RZ-R' and MH653/'RZ-U', piloted by Fg Offrs H. Cogman and J. V. Macdonald respectively, soar above the dark lava slopes of Mount Vesuvius in the early afternoon of 27 January 1944. MH653 was usually Flt Lt A. M. S. Steedman's aircraft: he was flying it on 11 February when the engine failed and he had to make a crash-landing on the Vesuvius strip. The Squadron did not have the red theatre-colour spinners at this time. (IWM)

Far left, top LAC Wally Passmore (left) and AC Jim Birkett work on a No 241 Squadron Merlin on a chilly day in January 1944. The winter weather in southern Italy was in sharp contrast to the North African climate experienced the previous year. (IWM)

Left, top Fg Off W. R. B. McMurray, a No 241 Squadron pilot. (IWM)

Left, bottom Halifax II BB331 of No 614 Squadron at Amendola, Italy, May 1943. Two dozen raid symbols are painted below the cockpit, all but one of these operations having been undertaken with No 178 Squadron and later No 462 Squadron RAAF (which had been the unit title of No 614 Squadron until 3 March 1943, when it was re-numbered because British personnel were in the majority). (F. Bamberger)

Right, top The diverse RAF Commands in the Mediterranean area included a coastal organization with a role much as Coastal Command, albeit on a smaller scale. Wellingtons of No 221 Squadron were prominent in long-range patrols. Known as a 'Goofington' because of its sea-search radar antenna, Wellington XIII JA412 is here photographed on its way to drop supplies, including newspapers, leaflets and clothing, to isolated Greek towns cut off by the enemy's demolition of bridges. At the time No 221 Squadron was based at Hassani (Athens) and the date of the photograph is probably 27 February 1945. (IWM)

Right, bottom RAF West Africa was centred on Freetown and utilized a spread of airfields and flying-boat moorings in Gambia. The principal land-based unit was No 200 Squadron, which arrived in June 1941 with Lockheed Hudsons. Here a crew with a camera is about to emplane on Hudson 'K-King' for an anti-submarine patrol in March 1943. (IWM)

Left A No 200 Squadron Hudson, 'J-Jig', over a coastal region of Gambia in March 1943. (IWM)
Below Refuelling a Hudson with 100-octane fuel with the help of local labour. The Hudson had tankage for 950 US gallons, giving it a range of some 2,000 miles. (IWM)
Right, top An engine change on a Hudson at a West African base (probably Yundum) using an improvised hoist and native helpers. (IWM)
Right, bottom Shorts, sun hats and the shelter of a makeshift hangar made the airman's work more bearable in the African heat. Here the Allison engine of a Tomahawk has mass attention. This photograph is believed to have been taken at Takoradi. (IWM)

Tropical Tints

For the South-East Asia Theatre, with aircraft at bases in India and Ceylon and operating in Burma, the Temperate Land Camouflage Scheme was more functional than the Middle East Scheme. In Australia, too, and for the war in the South-West Pacific, the RAAF used the British camouflage colours for temperate climes, but with the additional colours of Foliage Green and Light Green when applying camouflage.

A significant difference in the appearance of service aircraft in these regions from mid-1942 was the exclusion of the red from the roundel, lest this style of national insignia be confused with the bright red 'rising sun' marking used by Japanese aircraft. The exclusion of red also applied to the fin flashes of the Royal Air Forces in these regions, viz. the RAF, RNZAF and RIAF.

Right, top Colour photographs of RAF subjects in the India/Burma war zones are particularly rare. This Thunderbolt II of No 30 Squadron is seen at Jumchar, India, on 15 January 1945. The fighter wears the special South-East Asia Command striping around the nose and tail surfaces, which served as a 'friendly' identification marking. Thunderbolts were the principal ground-attack fighters in the final months of operations against the Japanese, when fourteen squadrons were flying the type. (IWM)

Right, centre Photographic reconnaissance Spitfire XIs operating over Burma were flown by No 681 Squadron pilots. Here P Off L. G. Weber has put down at Monywa in PL969 'P-Peter' on 4 March 1945. A worn Hurricane and a dismembered Mosquito can be seen in the background. (Hank Redmond)

Far right, centre Silver or natural metal-finish aircraft had dark blue SEAC bands, as seen on Mosquito XVI NS787/'M' of No 684 Squadron. This photographic reconnaissance unit was based at Alipore, with detachments flying from several other airfields as required. NS787, nursing a 100-gallon auxiliary tank under each wing, was photographed *circa* March 1945 with Flt Lt C. G. Andrews, a New Zealander, at its controls. (IWM)

Right, bottom RAAF combat units operating in New Guinea and the Netherlands East Indies against the Japanese were mostly equipped with US aircraft types. However, RAAF fighter squadrons and No 54 Squadron RAF, charged with the defence of western and northern Australia, were equipped with Spitfires, and two of these units moved to Morotai early in 1945. The photograph was taken at an airstrip on that island early in 1945 and shows Foliage Green Spitfire VIIIs of No 79 Squadron RAAF. (Don Soderlund)

Training Yellow

Yellow was the predominant colour for training aircraft. In the International Flag Code, yellow stood for 'Fever', implying 'Keep well away'—and the same applied to training aircraft. In Commonwealth countries most wartime trainers were painted yellow overall, but in the United Kingdom, within striking distance of the *Luftwaffe*, it was prudent to have the upper and side surfaces in the standard Temperate Land Scheme of green and brown, not only for concealment on the ground but also to make them less conspicuous to marauding enemy aircraft making use of cloud cover to intrude over Britain.

From mid-1944 certain trainer types in Britain were permitted to have their wing tips boldly marked in the conspicuous yellow over the camouflaged upper surface, high visibility in order to reduce the number of collisions having by then become more important than concealment from the enemy—again, a case of colours indicating the course of the air war.

While operational aircraft usually had plain under surfaces, training and communications aircraft had their serial identity marked on the wing under surfaces (on the lower wing in the case of biplanes), reading opposite ways on port and starboard sides. This was so that ground observers could report cases of irresponsible low flying and to deter trainees from indulging in just that by the knowledge that their numbers could be taken.

It should be appreciated that yellow did not apply to all training units, but mainly to those concerned with the early stages of flying training: Operational Training Units came under operational Commands, using aircraft types common to that Command and finished in the same way.

Right, top The Airspeed Oxford I was the standard twin-engine trainer throughout the war period and the type on which most multi-engine RAF pilots trained in the United Kingdom. Those shown were serving with No 6 Service Flying Training School (SFTS) at Little Rissington, Gloucestershire, when photographed on either 12 or 13 February 1943. The aircraft nearest the camera, T1244, had long service, including a period with the USAAF at Bovingdon and Alconbury from April to November 1944. (IWM)

Right, bottom To meet its huge requirement for air crews, the RAF arranged for training to be carried out under the Empire Air Training Scheme at installations in the Commonwealth, notably in Canada, Australia, New Zealand, South Africa and Rhodesia. Additionally, flight training for 16,000 men was conducted in the United States, initially under the so-called Arnold Scheme when that country was still neutral. Primary training was carried out at six private flying schools under contract to the USAAF. This is the presentation of diplomas by Mr Paul Riddle to cadets of the first course, Class 42-B, at Embry-Riddle Company, Carlstrom Field, Arcadia, Florida on 16 August 1941. Part of the first course of 99, who started on 7 June 1941, these cadets wear the white flash identifying air crew trainees in their caps. Shirts and trousers are USAAC issue. L. J. Povey was the Company's General Manager. (IWM)

133

Left, top RAF cadets take a break from the hot Florida sun beside Stearman PT-17 primary trainers supplied by the USAAF and resplendent in that Service's bright yellow and blue trainer colours. (IWM)

Left, centre Cadets with seat parachutes and their American instructors (white flying suits) prepare to take to the air at Riddle Field, June 1941. The course consisted of 60 hours' instruction and those qualifying were sent on for 70 hours' basic and then 70 hours' advanced training at other US establishments. (IWM)

Left, bottom During the Second World War more flying personnel for the RAF and Commonwealth air forces were trained in Canada than in all other countries combined if the United Kingdom is excluded. As elsewhere, the trusty North American Harvard was the standard trainer for advanced tuition. The first for the Royal Canadian Air Force was RCAF No 3560, taken on charge on 19 September 1940 and used by the Central Flying School, Trenton, Ontario, until damaged on 17 July 1941. Thereafter it became a static instructional airframe. Photographed here before delivery, the Harvard sports a number based on its US civil registration. (Peter Bowers)

Right, top 'Faithful Annie'. Avro Anson I 6054 of the RCAF was built in Britain for the RAF (as R3533) but shipped straight from production to Canada. In trainer dress it served at No 4 Bombing and Gunnery School, Fingal, Ontario, for most of the war. (I. Dmitri)

Right, bottom The South African Air Force took RAF cadets for air crew training under the Commonwealth Joint Air Training Plan. No 23 Air School at Waterkloof, Pretoria, formed in June 1941, was one such installation and used an assortment of aircraft types. Some SAAF women worked as fitters, as seen here servicing Hawker Hart 2057 in January 1943. (IWM)

Left, top No 23 Air School trained air gunners. Pupils waiting to take a turn in the power turret rig could not have been very comfortable wearing full flying clothes and gloves in the African heat. The target was a motorized rail buggy which orbited a track at around 40mph. Ammunition was replenished by the Askari orderlies, who also gathered cases from fired rounds. (IWM)

Left, bottom Air firing over a Rhodesian range involved a Fairey Battle towing a drogue sleeve while the student operated the power turret of Oxford AS515. Both aircraft were operated by No 24 Bombing, Gunnery and Navigation School at Moffat. Without the need for camouflage, trainers in South Africa could sport overall yellow colouring. This photograph was taken in January 1943. (IWM)

Right, top Advanced pilot instruction, a course lasting up to sixteen weeks, was usually carried out at a Service Flying Training School. No 20 SFTS was set up at Cranborne near Salisbury, Rhodesia, in July 1940 and the North American Harvard became its standard equipment. Here sixteen instructors (front row) and pupils parade with these aircraft in January 1943. (IWM)

Right, bottom Sgt D. H. Marshall enlisted in India and served as a ground crewman for 2½ years before being accepted for flight training. He is shown here entering Harvard '49' at Cranborne. (IWM)

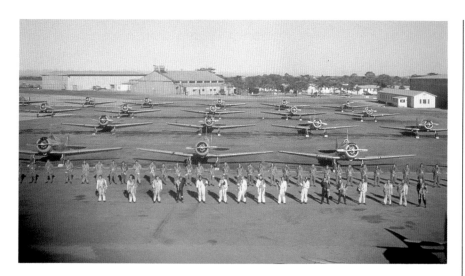

Left, top Harvard EX180 taxies out at Cranborne as another comes in to land. (IWM)

Left, bottom Harvard IIAs from No 20 SFTS, January 1943. EX375/'11' survived war service to go to No 4 Flying Training School (FTS) and was lost in a collision with another Harvard near Bulawayo on 18 May 1950 while serving with this unit. (IWM)

Right, top Native Rhodesians refuel Harvard '88' of No 20 SFTS at Kisumu in January 1943. (IWM)

Right, bottom Harvards of No 20 SFTS over Rhodesia, January 1943. The leading aircraft have all-yellow paintwork, a scheme discontinued on later arrivals which retained their natural metal finishes. (IWM)

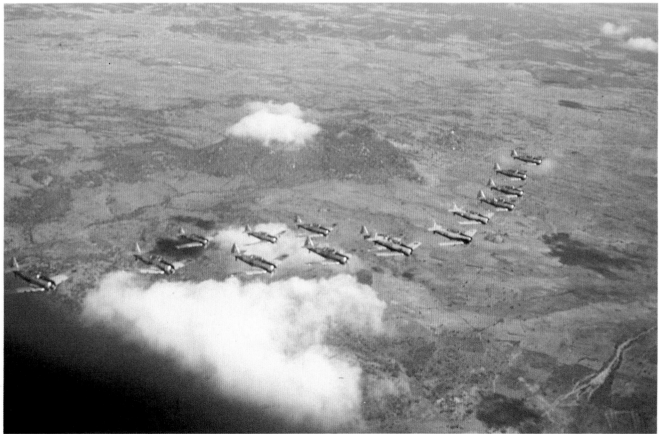

Left, top No 2 (Indian) Elementary Flying Training School at Jodhpur, India, was initially equipped with Tiger Moths taken over in 1940 from eight flying clubs in the Sub-Continent. DG518, shown, was one of those impressed into the Indian Air Force. On the post-war partition of India, this Tiger Moth went to the Royal Pakistan Air Force. (IAF)

Left, centre The Empire Central Flying School at Hullavington, Wiltshire, provided instruction for test pilots and other specialist requirements. A variety of service types were on hand, often those aircraft that had been retired from first-line service. Of this mixed formation photographed on 16 September 1942, Hurricane I Z4791 spent practically its whole existence serving in a training capacity, in contrast to the two Spitfire IIs which served with several fighter squadrons over two years. The nearest Spitfire, P7926, is the presentation aircraft *Hereward the Wake*; it had previously served with Nos 610, 130, 411, 121 and 340 Squadrons and with No 53 Operational Training Unit. The furthest Spitfire is P7882, which had flown with Nos 152, 134 and 312 Squadrons and from the ECFS passed to No 53 OTU at Hibaldstow, where it undershot while coming in to land on 4 May 1944. (RAF Museum)

Left, bottom A Hawker Henley reposing at Cranwell in the late summer of 1939. Originally designed as a light bomber, the Henley fell victim to Air Ministry disenchantment with this role and the 200 built were completed as tugs for towing gunnery targets. L3295 has the black diagonal bars that distinguished aircraft so committed. After service with many units, this Henley was written off in a forced landing at Bentley, Suffolk, on 18 June 1943. (AVM M. D. Lyne)

Right, top The Miles Martinet TT.1 was specifically developed from the Master trainer for target-towing duties, 1,724 being built for this purpose between 1943 and 1945. Here HN862, the second production aircraft, displays the diagonal black and yellow underwing stripes that identify target-towing aircraft. After evaluation trials with the Royal Aircraft Establishment, this Martinet was wrecked in a forced landing at Muston, Yorkshire, while serving with No 1634 Flight. (RAF Museum)

Right, bottom The Central Gunnery School at Sutton Bridge had a complement of aircraft that included most types currently serving with operational commands. Wellington IA N2887, photographed here on 24 June 1943 flying south-east of Chatteris, started out with No 99 Squadron at Mildenhall. Retired from operations, it went on to serve with Nos 11 and 15 OTUs and the Air Armament School before seeing service with the CGS at Sutton Bridge, where it stayed from 6 April 1942 to 23 February 1944. The aircraft was then dispatched to the Far East, where it finished its days and was SOC on 26 April 1945. (RAF Museum)

TRAINING YELLOW

Production Painting

Aircraft of the RAF emerged from the factories in the colours appropriate to the role for which they had been contracted. The colours and finished scheme were notified by charts and directives from the Ministry of Aircraft Production, who also specified durability standards for dopes and paints, application methods and the number of coatings. To follow the disruptive patterning of the two-tone camouflage schemes, charts would show measurements from key location points so that the pattern could be chalked on the aircraft for the spray painters who had to ensure that the colours merged one into the other.

From production, after final inspection and test flying, aircraft were ferried by ATA to locations decreed by the Air Ministry. Many went to Maintenance Units for storage as reserve or to be shipped or flown to ferrying units for overseas commands; or shipped as 'exports', like nearly 3,000 Hurricanes sent as aid to Russia. Others were prepared for RAF service with specialist equipment, particularly AI and ASV radars; because such items were highly secret and would be betrayed by attached and projecting antennae, any photography of them would be banned or doctored by the censor. The delivery of the aircraft to their allotted service unit would again be a task for ATA. Quite often the same aircraft would be ferried more than once; for example, ATA made 57,826 ferry flights with Spitfires and Seafires although only around 20,000 were built during the period ATA was operating, 1939–45.

Right and overleaf Between 1939 and 1945 some 80,000 aircraft were built in the United Kingdom for the British Services, predominantly the RAF. Heavy bombers were a major programme, the Lancaster being built in the largest numbers (7,366). Those sectionally built at Avro's main Manchester plant were assembled at Woodford, where these two colour photographs were taken in the early summer of 1943. JB276 can be seen; this was a Lancaster with a short life for, delivered to No 103 Squadron in September that year, it was lost the following month on the night of 22/23 during a raid on Kassel. At their peak the group of factories producing Lancasters employed nearly 40,000 people. (IWM)

Left, top Lancasters were flight-tested at Woodford or Ringway from dawn to dusk, seven days a week, and this necessitated employing several test crews. Only one accident claimed the lives of the test crew during the whole programme. Here, photographed from nearby Poynton, a Lancaster returns to Woodford on a wild spring evening in 1945. (Ted Wurm)

Left, bottom DH test pilot John de Havilland checks the flight log with fitters at Hatfield in May 1943. He was killed in a flying accident on 23 August the same year. (IWM)

Right, top Final assembly of Mosquitos at Hatfield from mostly wooden components manufactured by a large number of small companies. At the time of this photograph, autumn 1943, different models were being produced in batches on the same assembly lines. A Mosquito FB.VI, LR264, can be seen and this served with Nos 613, 107 and 69 Squadrons before being SOC in October 1945. The PR.IX, MM256, was not so fortunate: delivered in November 1943 to No 60 Squadron SAAF, it was missing over Marseilles on 13 May 1944. A total of 7,781 Mosquitos were produced. (IWM)

Right, bottom Final checks on Mosquito HJ728 before a test flight from Hatfield. Delivered to No 301 Ferry Training Unit, the aircraft was later sent to the Mediterranean where it served first with No 23 Squadron and then with No 108 Squadron, from where it was reported Missing in Action on 6 May 1944. (IWM)

PRODUCTION PAINTING

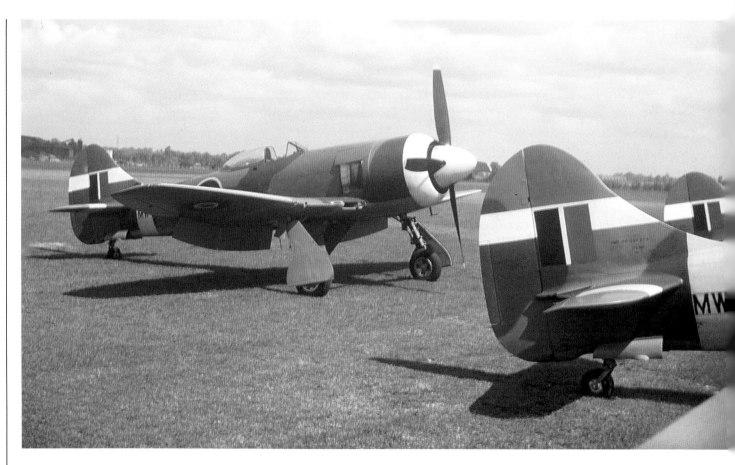

Left, top Tempest IIs awaiting delivery at Hawker's Langley factory airfield in March 1945. The white tail and nose bands are markings for operations in South-East Asia, where it was planned that these aircraft would be sent to replace the Thunderbolts used by squadrons operating in the India/Burma area. (IWM)

Left, bottom Taylorcraft Aeroplanes (England) Ltd produced the Auster, which was classified as an Air Observation Post although its primary use was as an artillery spotter. It was a military adaption of a pre-war civilian sports plane. The manufacturers were out to impress Charles Brown when he visited their flying field and part works at Rearsby on 27 March 1944 by getting a young lady to demonstrate how easily the rear end could be lifted. Shown is MT225, an AOP.IV, which later served with No 659 Squadron; MS935, in the background, eventually joined No 653 Squadron. (RAF Museum)

Right, top By arrangement with the Ministry of Aircraft Production, aircraft manufacturers retained certain of their products for experimental work. For a time this early Halifax I served such a purpose at Handley Page's Leavesden factory airfield. The bomber is seen over Kings Langley in June 1943. (IWM)

Right, centre The delivery of aircraft from factories and Maintenance Units was largely undertaken by the ATA, ostensibly a civilian organization although dependent on the RAF in many areas of its operations. ATA included a large number of highly competent women pilots. One of these ladies is seen here in the cockpit of Anson N5060, which was used to collect and deliver pilots. (RAF Museum)

Right, bottom Prototypes were initially identified by a marking comprising a yellow 'P' in a circle, as on this Percival Proctor IV, LA589; this was to denote that no instructional manual was available. The photograph was taken by Charles Brown on 10 August 1943. This second prototype of the Mk IV, when its test work was completed, went on to serve with the Bristol Wireless Flight and finally the Station Flight at Halton before being sold for civilian use. (RAF Museum)

Left, top A line-up of Proctors at Percival's airfield at Luton. NP229 was a production Mk IV built by F. Hills and Sons of Manchester, LA586 was the Percival-built prototype of the Mk IV and DX198 was a Hills-built Mk III. A total of 1,143 Proctors were built during the Second World War for communications and training use. About a quarter of Britain's total aircraft production was devoted to training and light communications types. (RAF Museum)

Left, centre In addition to its own production, Britain received many thousands of military aircraft from the United States, mostly through the Lend-Lease scheme. One design specially built to a British order was the North American Mustang, later developed into the best long-range fighter of the war. AG346 was the second production Mustang and is seen here before a test flight at Inglewood, California, early in 1941. Among the first batch shipped to Britain, AG346 gave excellent service and was eventually shot down by flak while serving with No 168 Squadron on 20 August 1944. (S. Clay)

Left, bottom One of the earliest types obtained from the United States was the Douglas DB-7 light bomber, which was used by British and Commonwealth squadrons throughout hostilities in Europe and the Mediterranean war zones as the Boston. AL399, seen here on a test flight from Douglas Aircraft's Santa Monica factory in California, never reached Britain for, like many others of its kind, it was diverted to the USAAF when America suddenly found itself in hostilities. (MOI)

Right, top Although one RAF fighter squadron, No 601, was re-armed with the Bell Airacobra, the type's performance was considered too poor for fighter operations from the United Kingdom. The remainder of the British allocation went straight to the USSR. AH435, seen here on a demonstration flight from Bell's Buffalo, New York, factory airfield, was one that went to Russia. The Soviets put Airacobras to good use in ground attack and the type proved popular with pilots. This aircraft was unusual in that the engine was positioned aft of the cockpit, the propeller being driven by an extended power shaft. (USAAF)

Right, bottom The first production aircraft of most types went to the Aeroplane and Armament Experimental Establishment at Boscombe Down for handling trials. Vampire TG274 was present there from July to October 1945. The Boscombe Down hangar line appears in this photograph. (IWM)

PRODUCTION PAINTING

Other Tinges

There were many Royal Air Force organizations that had no direct belligerent function or prominent flying role to attract photographers with rare colour film to expose. Even so, some such cover does exist of varied subjects, a selection of which follows. But again, the chief tool of the RAF's trade, the aeroplane, remained the main allure for the lens.

Right, top Flying Control was essential for the safe operation of aircraft, with the Watch Office, or Control Tower, the hub of airfield flying control. One of the busiest in the United Kingdom was at Prestwick, where many transatlantic flights started or terminated. The controllers in the tower had an American visitor when this photograph was taken. White Coastal Command Liberators can be seen on the airfield. (IWM)

Right, bottom Balloon Command received meagre publicity compared with Commands operating aircraft, yet at its peak there were over 2,000 balloons in place controlled by more than fifty squadrons. The original object of balloon defences was to deter low-level and dive-bombing attacks on vulnerable target areas, but with the launching of the V-1 flying bombs from the Pas de Calais area in June 1944 a large proportion of the balloon force was re-located across the south-eastern approaches to London. During this campaign some 231 V-1s were credited as having been brought down by balloons. The site in this photograph, taken by Fg Off W. Bellamy on 5 July 1944, is a Kent field not far from Biggin Hill. (IWM)

Left, top to bottom No 1426 (Enemy Aircraft) Flight based at Collyweston, adjacent to Wittering, had a variety of captured enemy types used for comparison testing with Allied aircraft and for recognition training. Ju 88A-5 No 6067, M2+MK of *Küstenfliegergruppe* 106, landed in error at Chivenor owing to the disorientation of the crew on 26 November 1941. Painted for British service—although the individual letter 'M' was retained on the fuselage—it was also given the serial HM509. The aircraft is seen in flight (top) over Northamptonshire in the summer of 1943. Another long-time assignee to No 1426 Flight was He 111H No 6353, which, in RAF service, flew as AW177 (second photograph). Acquired after being attacked by Spitfires, causing it to belly-land near Haddington, Scotland, on 28 October 1939, this Heinkel was repaired and flown for evaluation. In RAF service it retained the *Luftwaffe* unit's shield on the left side of the nose. (USAAF)

The Telecommunications Flying Unit (TFU), based at Defford, carried out the flying requirements of the Telecommunications Research Establishment (TRE) at nearby Malvern. It frequently had more than a dozen different aircraft types at hand, ranging from four-engine heavy bombers through amphibians and single-engine fighters to light biplanes. Most were used to test experimental radar equipment developed by TRE. The photograph of a TFU Beaufighter I was taken from the unit's Lancaster. (Douglas Fisher)

Supermarine Walrus L2201 of the Telecommunications Flying Unit (bottom), photographed from a Swordfish over Lough Foyle in January 1943. The aircraft was engaged in filming simulated attacks on a Royal Navy submarine for the purpose of making a training device to improve Coastal Command depth-charge attacks on diving U-boats. On these sorties this Fleet Air Arm aircraft carried on RAF pilot, an RAF signaller, a WRNS wireless operator, a civilian TRE senior scientific officer and a civilian TRE photographer; the last, Douglas Fisher, who operated a hand-held 16mm camera while kneeling and exposed to the 100mph-plus slipstream, can be seen in the nose of the Walrus. (Douglas Fisher)

Right, top The RAF had its own specialized hospitals and convalescent centres which were staffed by RAF medical personnel and those of Princess Mary's RAF Nursing Service. Here patients are enjoying the sunshine on 27 August 1943 at Halton Hospital, which was opened by Princess Mary in October 1927. (IWM)

Right, bottom Towards the end of hostilities consideration was given to the rehabilitation of large numbers of RAF personnel who would soon be returned to civilian life. RAF Resettlement Training Centres were set up to provide education and instruction for post-war employment opportunities. Manchester Central Library was one venue, where the mixed class in this photograph are receiving mathematics tuition. Rulers, pencils and exercise books must have been evocative of school days. (IWM)

OTHER TINGES

Indexes

INDEX OF AIRCRAFT TYPES

INDEX OF PERSONNEL

Right The high losses of Bomber Command are illustrated by the fate of these three Lancaster Is of No 44 Squadron, photographed on 29 September 1942. W4125 (being flown here by Sgt Colin Watt, an Australian, and his crew) went missing on the Munich raid of 21/22 December 1942 with Fg Off D. F. Biggane and crew. W4162/'KM-Y' survived for 399 flying hours before being lost with Flt Sgt R. Brown and crew of No 460 Squadron RAAF on 23/24 November 1943 (it was one of twenty Lancasters lost against Berlin that night. In the photograph the aircraft is being flown by P Off T. G. Hackney, a Rhodesian, and crew, who went missing on 6/7 November 1942 while serving with No 83 Squadron. W4277/'KM-S' is here in the hands of M. J. Paige and crew; both crew and aircraft were lost on a mining sortie on 8/9 January 1943. Only Sgt Watt and his crew survived their tour. (IWM)

INDEX OF PLACENAMES

INDEX OF UNITS